I

EUROPE AND THE WORLD

IN ROMAN TIMES, THE MEDITER-
ranean was a Latin lake, and England was the northern tip of
civilization. It was the same at the end of the Middle Ages. Learning,
science, commerce, banking, mathematics and shipping were developed on the coasts of the intercontinental sea. There Southern Europe
met North Africa and the Middle East, the gateway to Asia. Jerusalem,
the Holy City of Christians and Muslims and Jews, was the symbol of
the encounter of the three continents, the centre of the world. From
the time of the classical Greeks, the Mediterranean had been the basin
of culture, only open to the western ocean between the Pillars of
Hercules, now called the Strait of Gibraltar.

The Atlantic then was important as a mere strip of sea bordering
the stormy coasts linking Mediterranean trade to the ports of Portugal
and France and England and the Baltic. The Pacific Ocean, too, was
a commercial extension of the Red Sea and the Persian Gulf. Along
the shores of Africa and over to India and the spice islands of the East
Indies, Arab dhows cruised with their lateen sails. Their galleys also
fought the Christian fleets in the Mediterranean. Their charts and
skills in navigation and shipbuilding spread. From the East came
instruction in the use of geometry and trigonometry and astronomy,
of the astrolabe and the star calendar, and in the calculation of latitude
by the cross-staff, called the *kamal*. This transfer of technology was a
dangerous gift, for the new sea powers of Europe wanted to break the
Arab monopoly on the spice and gold trade of Africa and Asia. Vasco
da Gama himself was first piloted across the Indian Ocean by its
leading navigator, Ahmed bin Majid, whose brass quadrants were
superior to da Gama's great wooden astrolabe.

Although the medieval Portuguese seemed only semi-civilized to
refined Arabs, and barbarian to the Chinese, who condescended to
these 'sea-robbers', their voyages and discoveries were to set the

A cross-staff used in sighting the Pole Star, 1545.
From Pedro de Medina's Arte de Navegar.

urban culture of Europe against the forest cultures of West Africa and the Americas. In this shock, European expansion was to be borne on the yellow gold of commerce and defended by the walls of wooden ships and colonial fortresses. These outposts of Europe, moving across the ocean or fixed on the fringes of continents, encouraged and paid for the growth of the small cities of the motherland. In the way that Venice had grown, through the trade of the Levant, from some marsh villages into a stone trading metropolis set on logs in its lagoon, so Portuguese Sagres was to rise on the commerce of Africa and the spice islands, while Spanish Cadiz was to flourish on the profits from the Americas.

The discoverers carried the expectations of Europe as cargo in their minds. They saw what they already believed. Columbus himself brought the ideas of the Old World to draw in the lines of the New.

The encounter of Vespucci with the Brazilian Indians.
From a German engraving, 1509.

Not only could the map-makers now begin to chart the shores of the
western continents, but philosophers and priests could describe
native societies in terms of a golden age and of heaven and hell. The
letter which Columbus sent back to Spain about the New World made
it seem an earthly paradise, nearer to dream than discovery. Among
the nightingales and green fields and metal mines, the natives were
naked and innocent. 'They are so guileless and so generous with all
they possess, that no one would believe it who has not seen it.'
Amerigo Vespucci, whose Christian name became the name of the
new continents, agreed, finding that the natives of Brazil lived for
pleasure and the delights of the senses.

Such simple visions could not endure. If there were to be colonies
and empires, the natives had to be displaced and enslaved. Instead of
seeming people from a golden age, they now appeared to be

The Indians in Brazil before the arrival of Amerigo Vespucci and the Portuguese fleet. From a German engraving, 1505.

barbarians and devils in the ferocity of their resistance. The clash of Iberian and Indian in the Americas confirmed the worst fears of both cultures. The inhuman greed of the Europeans was matched by the human sacrifices of the Aztecs. Ignored was the lasting benefit of the encounter in terms of the exchange of ideas and technology, goods and products.

The Elizabethan venturers and colonists would go through the same process of discovery in their turn. England was formally excluded from the benefits of the New World. A Spanish Pope split all territories unknown to Europe between the two leading maritime powers: the Americas, except for Brazil, were granted to Spain, the rest to Portugal. So the merchants and sailors of the West of England found themselves prohibited from access to the rich trade in precious metals and silk and spices. They dreamed of discovering a direct north-western route to China, which would avoid the Spanish empire in Middle and South America.

The merchants of Bristol found themselves an explorer, John Cabot of Genoa and Venice, to lead their quest. He was granted a royal

Spanish navigators using the cross-staff and astrolabe, c. *1557.*
From a contemporary woodcut.

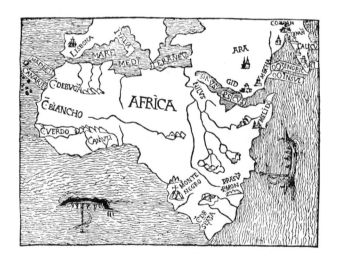

A woodcut map of Africa and the route to India, 1508.
From the Itinerarium Portugallensium.

patent, giving him a trade monopoly in any virgin territories he might find. He discovered the rich fishing-grounds off Newfoundland, while his son Sebastian probably reached Hudson Bay in an effort to prove the North-West Passage to Asia. Sebastian Cabot later became Pilot-Major of Spain with access to all its maritime secrets. He was bribed to return to England to teach navigation and the organization of trading companies such as the new Muscovy Company. He was the guiding spirit behind the expeditions that began establishing trade with Russia and Africa.

Before Queen Elizabeth's reign, the English contribution to the Age of Discovery was little. Only Roger Bacon, himself taught from Mediterranean science, prophesied a western voyage round the world to Asia. Two centuries later, his theories were copied in the *Imago Mundi*, which inspired Columbus to begin his voyage to the Caribbean. In spite of the probes of the Cabots, there was no effort by the English to found colonies or bases in North America. The building of a Royal Navy by the Tudor kings and the founding of Trinity House as a school of navigation showed interest in the mastery of the sea. But this was only a prelude to innovation and expansion.

II

YOUTH

I<small>N THE MIDDLE OF THE SIXTEENTH</small> century, England was still a forest with flocks of sheep on the cleared lands and downs, three times as many sheep as the three million people who hardly filled the kingdom. Round the villages there were strips of ploughland and commons, not yet enclosed into fields. Only London was large; perhaps 300,000 people lived there; the other cities held no more than 20,000. Travel was at the pace of a slow horse. It was a week's ride from the capital to Cornwall. Water was the quickest route: even Oxford and Cambridge considered themselves as ports because transport by river was more secure than by road. The sea was the highway and the opportunity of the island off Europe, the hope and the future.

Yet the forests were falling because of the need of wood for ships and houses, for heating and for industry. By the end of the Tudor century, England was already looking overseas for timber for its fleets. Outside the ports, the village and the market town and the county were the limits of the perception of the world. London seemed a far and foreign place to much of the island, while the Court was as distant as heaven. Queen Elizabeth I herself never progressed further north than Derby or further west than Bristol, although she reigned over all England.

Although life was not short of food or work, its expectation was half the modern span. The young rose quickly and did not make old bones. Disease and violence were common, and death and risk part of the running of the days. Above all, there was a sense of the drama of existence in an age when the theatre fed popular taste with its heightened show of reality. Self-assertion and national pride made Elizabethan England into a thrusting culture, sure of its own worth and prepared to fly its standards abroad. Walter Raleigh was born with a nascent character that would suit his country and his time.

His actual year of birth is uncertain, probably 1552, six years before the accession of Queen Elizabeth to the throne. He was the younger of two sons of a Devon squire, also named Walter Raleigh, by a third marriage. His mother, Katherine Champernowne, had been married once before and already had three sons, one of whom was Humphrey Gilbert. The young Walter Raleigh was related to many of the leading families of the West Country interested in discovery and sea trading and raiding – the Gilberts and the Grenvilles, the Russells and the Courtenays, the Drakes and the Carews. The Raleighs were a Protestant family; the father had been nearly hanged during a local Catholic uprising and, during the persecutions when Mary Tudor was Queen, the mother had visited one of the Protestant martyrs in Exeter Castle before she was burned alive. The young Walter was brought up to hate Philip of Spain and the Catholic powers and to love the sea and its opportunities. His mother's brother was Vice-Admiral of Devon, and tales of adventure by sea were part of his boyhood.

Younger sons of the gentry without an inheritance could rise through influence at Court, a good marriage, the law, or war on land or sea. At the age of sixteen, Raleigh went up to Oriel College at Oxford University, where his brilliance and his poverty were soon known. His wit was always quick. A friend, challenged to a duel, was good at the bow and bad at the sword: Raleigh advised him to settle for a shooting match at a distance. Soon he himself tired of formal study and set off for the religious wars in France. One of his cousins, Gawain Champernowne, had married the daughter of the Count de Montgomerie, a Huguenot leader. A force of 100 horsemen was raised in Devon to fight under de Montgomerie's black banner, which carried a severed head and the motto, VALOUR BE MY END. If captured, the men of Devon would be hanged and valour would be their end. For Queen Elizabeth had officially disclaimed the English volunteers, while secretly supporting their intervention.

The Devon troop of horse arrived in France only to join the retreat of the defeated Huguenot army. They fought in a rearguard action, where Raleigh learned to admire the courage and strategy of Coligny, the Admiral of France who had first sent colonists to North America. Coligny survived defeat after defeat, yet held together the remnants of his army and raised a new one. He eventually forced a truce on his royal and Catholic opponents, the prelude to his own death at the Massacre of St Bartholomew's Day. The Count de Montgomerie also

Jean Ribaut's French expedition of 1562 approaching South Carolina.
From Theodore de Bry's Indorum Floridam provinciam inhabitantium . . ., *1591.*

met the end predicted on his black banner: he was betrayed and beheaded.

Raleigh learned terrible lessons during his four years of fighting in the French religious wars. He called them civil wars and commented that no nation was ever bettered by them. He saw terror and counter-terror, broken faith and ruse, savagery and no nobility. After a calculated campaign of destruction, a marshal of France confessed that 'if the mercies of God were not infinite, none of his profession could expect any'. Blow for blow, the Huguenots gave no quarter to their Catholic enemies, who were butchered after being smoked out of caves like bees from a hive. Raleigh learned how ruthlessness was the best policy in war, and how bold, persistent leadership was necessary at all times. This was the price of survival.

After returning briefly to Oriel College, Raleigh enrolled in the Middle Temple, one of the Inns of Court. A fair knowledge of the law was considered essential for a country landowner: it was the equiv-alent of war, the way to protect property against all comers. But Raleigh, a veteran soldier in his early twenties without any property, had nothing to protect and boasted that he never read any law at all – a failing that was to cost him his life when he defended himself at his treason trials.

Raleigh was over six feet tall, a head higher than most of his contemporaries. He was thin and strong, forceful and incisive, with a vast forehead and a beard with natural curl. If there was a defect in his handsome figure and face, it was his narrow eyes, always seeking advantage. He was proud of his harsh Devon accent, which demon-strated his roots and connections. He was, as John Aubrey wrote, 'a person so much immersed in action all along, and in fabrication of his own Fortunes' that he had little time for study. Yet, at that, 'he was no Slug. Without doubt he had a wonderful waking spirit, and a great judgment to guide it.'

His pride was his weakness. Twice he went briefly to prison for duelling. Once he literally sealed a tavern bore's mouth by pouring hot wax on the man's moustaches and beard. His dress was rich and flamboyant; he insisted on drawing attention to himself as the chief actor in the drama of his life. Through his half-brother, Humphrey Gilbert, he met his ideal, the swashbuckling poet George Gascoigne, a veteran of the Flanders wars and the courtly pen. Gascoigne had fought disastrously under Gilbert in the Netherlands and now helped his old commander to publish a book that tried to prove the existence

The Queen receiving the poet George Gascoigne. From a contemporary engraving.

of the North-West Passage to China. Gilbert used Sebastian Cabot's explorations to assert that there was a 'Strait of Anian' above Canada that led down to the Pacific Ocean. The patron of a venturer bold enough to sail that strait would make himself rich and the world happy. Gilbert was backed in his assertions by John Dee, an ingenious mathematician and astrologer, who had taken Cabot's place as the chief instructor of the English captains in navigation and discovery.

The search for the North-West Passage would become the dominant theme in English exploration for the next fifty years. Gilbert's false reasoning was received as gospel truth. The hope of the China route was held to be the fact. Letters patent from the Crown were granted to Gilbert in 1578 for a period of six years, giving him the sole right to explore and settle colonies in America. Scouting expeditions by Martin Frobisher had seemed to confirm both the entrance to the North-West Passage and the existence of black stone that contained traces of gold. Now Gilbert used his West Country connections to

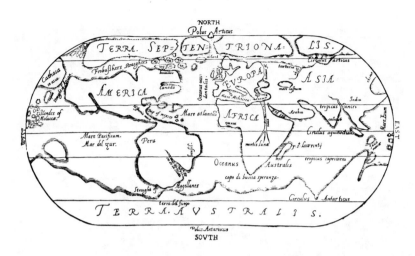

A map of the world showing the Frobisher Straits leading to China, 1578.
From George Best, True Discourse . . .

raise and victual a fleet of ten small, well-armed ships. The destination
of the little fleet was not disclosed. Perhaps it was meant to found a
colony in the New World, but more probably to attack the riches of
the Spanish Main as Hawkins and Drake had been doing for many
years. Raleigh himself was given his first command of the Queen's
ship, the *Falcon*: his post suggests that he was already reckoned at
Court because of another Champernowne cousin, Katherine Ashley,
close to Her Majesty.

Gilbert was usually an unlucky commander. Three of his ships
deserted to go on a privateering foray of their own. Storms drove the
other seven ships back to Dartmouth harbour and finally prevented
them from crossing the Atlantic. Raleigh sailed off on the *Falcon*, fell
in with some Spanish ships on the way to the West Indies, and was
beaten in a fierce fight. He brought back a damaged royal ship: he was
liable for the necessary repairs. The two minor prizes seized by the
whole expedition were ordered to be returned to their owners by the
Privy Council, and Gilbert and Raleigh were put on surety not to
engage in piracy any more.

The failure of this expedition was contradicted the following year
by Francis Drake's return from sailing round the world, his small

English soldiers returning from fighting the Irish, 1581.
From John Derricke, The Image of Ireland.

ship so stacked with rich prizes that the golden dreams of the West
Countrymen were fired again. Drake's success, however, was of no
help to Gilbert or to Raleigh. They were ordered to Ireland, where
many of their Carew and Grenville relatives were colonists in
Munster, and where eleven years previously Gilbert had put down an
Irish rebellion with great brutality. Now the Desmond rebellion had
begun, aided by mercenaries from Spain and Italy, and Protestant
England seemed threatened in its undeclared war with Spain by a
Catholic attack from the west.

In fact, only 400 Catholic mercenaries reached the west coast of
Ireland. There they fortified Smerwick and waited for reinforcements
like rats in a trap. They were soon surrounded by an English army led
by Lord Grey de Wilton: Raleigh was one of his officers, commanding
100 foot soldiers. Siege guns battered the 500 defenders, who surrendered unconditionally according to the English. Lord Grey ordered
them all put to the sword. Raleigh's company was one of two
companies that carried out the execution.

In the French religious wars, Raleigh had seen the deliberate
massacre of eight times as many German prisoners. At Smerwick he
was responsible for carrying out his orders. Although a valid act of

A shepherd with his flock, 1579. From a woodcut in Edmund Spenser,
The Shepheardes Calender. *The poet Spenser was Lord Grey de Wilton's
assistant secretary on his Irish campaign.*

war at a time when religious fanaticism made Catholics and Protestants kill and torture their captives for their mistaken beliefs, this
massacre began a change in Raleigh. The inexcusable cruelty of
human beings to each other is a theme in his *History of the World*,
written during the thirteen years he lay under the shadow of death
in the Tower of London. He quoted Juvenal on the difference between
wanting to be merciful in war and having to be ruthless:

> Even they that have no murderous will,
> Would have it in their power to kill.

After Smerwick, Raleigh's exploits in Ireland told more of his
courage and spirit than his sense of survival. He fought his way out
of many ambushes, never leaving a man behind. With handfuls of his
own troops, he charged superior Irish forces and scattered them. He
tricked the ambiguous Lord Roche out of his castle and brought him
to Munster for questioning. He also intrigued for the gift of a forfeited
estate so that he could found a fortune. Yet finally, Irish guerrilla
tactics wore him down as they had so many other commanders
looking for quick victories. He wrote to the Earl of Leicester, the
Queen's favourite, that he would like a better assignment. He
disdained service in Ireland as much as keeping sheep. As for his

An Irish chief feasting, 1581. From John Derricke, The Image of Ireland.

superior officers and their policies, they were making Ireland 'a lost land – not a commonwealth, but a common woe'.

He was recalled to London to testify before the Privy Council about his difference with Lord Grey, who wanted to subjugate and colonize all Ireland. This policy was too expensive for the Queen. She listened to Raleigh's thrifty strategy, the Roman trick of dividing and ruling; the lesser Irish chiefs should be supported and protected in their own struggles against the oppression of the great Irish nobles. The Queen warmed to Raleigh's person and powers of persuasion as much as to his advice. His promotion was to be rapid, now that he had the chance to catch the Queen's eye and ear. 'He was one that it seems Fortune had picked out of purpose,' wrote an observer, Sir Robert Naunton, 'to use as her tennis ball.' Although Raleigh was rising by his own hard work and made his presence and talents further his opportunities, yet he was now 'tossed up from nothing, and to and fro to greatness'.

Queen Elizabeth I, c. 1559. By permission of the National Portrait Gallery.

III

THE QUEEN AND VIRGINIA

THE LEGENDS ABOUT RALEIGH'S involvement with Queen Elizabeth are dramatic truths. The Queen had a sense of theatre, and those who could play their parts greatly did well. Raleigh was a natural actor and courtier, for ever playing the soldierly swain to the Virgin Queen and the gallant adventurer to the pages of history. Ambitious and daring, brilliant and courageous, he could rise as far as the Queen allowed and fall overnight. He would provoke envy and admiration in other men, fortune and ruin for himself. As his very first poem noted:

> For whoso reaps renown above the rest,
> With heaps of hate shall surely be oprest.

The gossip of the time made him introduce himself to Queen Elizabeth by throwing his new plush cloak in the mud for her to tread on gently. The Queen then rewarded him 'with many suits'. Certainly, his fortunes changed dramatically. He received a commission to lead a larger company in Ireland, but as the Queen kept him at Court, he was allowed to sell the commission at a profit. He was given the lease of Durham House in the Strand, two estates from All Souls College, a patent on the sale of wines, a licence to export woollen cloth, and a knighthood to match Sir Francis Drake and his half-brother, Sir Humphrey Gilbert. From poverty and obscurity, the Queen translated him to riches and influence by her favour. Yet the man she made, she could unmake. Raleigh knew that only too well. His fear was inscribed in another reported scene, which had him scratching with a diamond on the glass of a palace window:

> Fain would I climb,
> Yet I fear to fall.

And the Queen cut with her diamond ring on the glass pane underneath:

> If thy heart fail thee,
> Climb not at all.

Raleigh's heart did not fail him, and he climbed into the Queen's counsel and affections. She called him her Oracle and, mimicking his accent, her 'Water' and her Shepherd of the Ocean. She used him to bind his network of West Country gentlemen firmly to the Crown. She made him Lord Warden of the Stannaries, responsible for regulating mining in Cornwall and Devon; later she created him Lord-Lieutenant of Cornwall and Vice-Admiral of the West. He was also elected a Member of Parliament for Devon in 1584. So Raleigh became the dominant power in the West Country as well as the Queen's own servant. She set the seal on her favour when she made him Captain of the Guard, so that he was always near her person in his silver armour or orange uniform of 'tawny medly', dripping with jewels.

The sudden rise of Raleigh led to the jealousy of the Queen's other favourites. As Naunton noted, when the Queen took Raleigh as her Oracle, she 'nettled them all'. The Earl of Leicester was ageing and his wife had died of a broken neck in suspicious circumstances. Sir Christopher Hatton might be rich, tall, handsome, and a fine dancer; but he was duller than Raleigh and lost his post of Captain of the Guard to his rival. The Duke d'Alençon was even a possible husband; but a foreign Consort was finally too dangerous to be considered. Now there was Raleigh, who knew how to woo the Queen in the poetic pastoral style as well as protecting her and giving her good advice. He addressed her as Diana, the virgin huntress, and Cynthia, goddess of the moon which ruled the ocean. He also flattered the ageing Queen as a woman. He praised her beauty and protested his passion for her. One of his poems to her declared:

> Those eyes which set my fancy on a fire,
> Those crisped hairs, which hold my heart in chains,
> Those dainty hands, which conquered my desire,
> That wit, which of my thoughts doth hold the reins!
>
> . . . Then Love be judge, what heart may thee withstand?
> Such eyes, such hair, such wit, and such a hand!

The Queen kept Raleigh close to her for ten years. All her advisers, including her Principal Secretary, William Cecil, Lord Burghley, had

Queen Elizabeth in the forest with her Court, 1575.
From George Turberville, The Book of Hunting.

to reckon with Raleigh's influence. Yet nobody doubted his loyalty or his zeal. Raleigh could 'toil terribly' – and he did in the Queen's service.

Raleigh was not only interested in western discovery through Sir Humphrey Gilbert, but also in shipbuilding and navigation. Noah's ark, he wrote, was the first ship, the invention of God himself. Raleigh praised the ark because it was capacious and strong enough to survive the rain and the Flood, when all other ships were wrecked. At his own cost from his new revenues, Raleigh built an improved warship, the *Ark Raleigh*, to sail with Gilbert on his next western expedition.

An English warship, probably the Ark Royal, *c. 1588.*

The *Ark Raleigh* had hardly left port with Gilbert's ships when it turned back, apparently full of contagious disease. Heavily in debt, Raleigh later lent his ship to the Queen, who made it into the flagship of her navy. She gave the *Ark Raleigh* the new name of the *Ark Royal* – to this day the proudest name in the British battle fleet.

There were six important elements in building a good ship for the Royal Navy: so Raleigh later taught Henry, Prince of Wales:

> First, That she be strong built.
> Secondly, That she be swift.
> Thirdly, That she be stout-sided.
> Fourthly, That she carry out her guns all weather.
> Fifthly, That she hull and try well, which we call a good sea-ship.
> Sixthly, That she stay well, when boarding and turning on a wind is required.

Raleigh's advice was sound, although Henry, Prince of Wales, would never live to build a Royal Navy as powerful as it was under Queen Elizabeth.

Raleigh aided the changes in marine design that made the English ships triumph over those of the Spanish and the Portuguese, the Genoans and the Venetians, the French and the upstart Dutch, as well as the galleys of the Mediterranean and the dhows and junks of the Pacific Ocean. Raleigh claimed that North Europeans had invented the compass, although much of navigational skill and many instruments had come to Europe from the Arab civilizations through Norman Sicily and Portugal and Spain to the maritime nations of the North Sea. 'Whosoever were the inventors,' Raleigh wrote with tact and truth, 'we find that every age had added somewhat to ships, and to all things else; and in my own time the shape of our English ships hath been greatly bettered.' He listed the improvements in English design: the chain pump, the striking of the top-mast, the weighing of anchors by capstans, four varieties of new sails, higher gun-decks to avoid the fate of the capsized *Mary Rose*, cross-pillars to strengthen ships and bear the weight of more cannon, and extended storm cables, 'for the length of the cable is the life of the ship in all extremities'.

Raleigh himself was responsible for certain advances in the art of navigation through his scientific interest and patronage of Thomas Hariot. Hariot acted as a mathematical adviser to Raleigh and his captains. He compiled a manual on navigation named the *Arcticon*, discovered the shadow-quadrant, corrected solar and star tables, and developed a true sea chart. Richard Hakluyt praised Raleigh for maintaining Hariot and allowing him to teach sea captains, so 'linking theory with practice, not without almost incredible results'. Raleigh was doing what the Portuguese and the Spanish had done, making

Shipbuilders calculating the design of a ship.
From Matthew Baker, Fragment of Ancient Shipbuilding.

it possible for science to serve in the mastery of the seas. Raleigh was also instrumental in introducing John Dee to the Queen, who eventually found him a post to pay for his mathematical studies. Raleigh always stressed the importance of the master mariners to his country. 'For whosoever commands the sea commands the trade; whosoever commands the trade of the world commands the riches of the world, and consequently the world itself.'

This foresight led Raleigh to oppose Spanish sea power all his life. He believed that the trade of England could not flourish except at the expense of Spain and its empire. There had been an undeclared sea war with Spain for many years. The Queen's grant of letters patent to Sir Humphrey Gilbert in North America denied Spanish claims to the whole continent. The aim was to make it English territory.

Before he left on his last voyage, the Queen gave Gilbert a token, an anchor guided by a lady. The token did not secure Gilbert. After annexing Newfoundland in the name of the Queen, Gilbert turned south. One of his larger vessels was wrecked on a sand-bar. He transferred from his flagship on to a pinnace, the *Squirrel*. This also sank in a storm on the voyage home, leaving the deathless image of

Gilbert reading the Bible on deck and crying out: 'We are as near to Heaven by sea as by land.' He had always been an unlucky captain. As Secretary Walsingham had said before his departure, Gilbert was 'noted of no good hap by sea'.

At the age of thirty and basking in the Queen's favour, Raleigh inherited Gilbert's endeavours. His half-brother's letters patent and viceregal powers over a new colony were granted to him. He was permitted 'to discover search find out and view such remote heathen and barbarous lands countries and territories not actually possessed of any Christian Prince'. Raleigh chose two captains from his household, Amadas and Barlowe, and sent them out in two small barks on a reconnaissance led by Gilbert's experienced Portuguese pilot, Simon Fernandez. They reached the West Indies, then sailed north. They landed in North Carolina near the island of the Roanoke Indians, an Algonquin-speaking tribe which received them well. Barlowe reported that the land was fertile in game, fish and crops – maize could be grown and harvested three times a year. 'The soil is the most plentiful, sweet, fruitful and wholesome of all the world.'

This was the land that Verrazzano had earlier named Arcadia after the earthly paradise of the Greeks – and Raleigh was to christen Virginia in honour of the Queen who had granted it to him. Richard Hakluyt, who wrote up the discoveries and promoted new colonies, penned for Raleigh a *Discourse Concerning Western Planting*, stating that Virginia could become another Mexico for England, providing tropical fruits, sugar, mulberry trees for silkworms, timber and marine supplies, and metals, as well as all its riches in food and game and fish. There would be no trouble with the local Indians, who seemed, as they had first seemed to Columbus, to be innocent and hospitable in their savage Garden of Eden. 'We found the people most gentle, loving and faithful,' Barlowe reported, 'void of all guile and treason, and such as lived after the manner of the golden age. The earth bringeth forth all things in abundance, as in the first creation, without toil or labour.'

When the reconnaissance expedition returned with two local Indians, Manteo and Wanchese, English relations with Spain were deteriorating. Ambassadors were withdrawn, and Queen Elizabeth began to permit attacks on Spanish shipping. Raleigh did not want to delay his colonizing venture in case his fleet was ordered to remain behind to defend the English coasts. The Queen herself lent Raleigh her *Tiger* as a flagship, and some gunpowder. Raleigh sent out his

The Tiger. *From Public Record Office, M.P.F. 75.*

own *Roebuck* to take prizes in the Channel in order to help pay for the costs of the expedition of seven vessels in all. Forbidden by the Queen to sail to Virginia himself, Raleigh put his cousin Sir Richard Grenville in charge, with Fernandez as his pilot. Ralph Lane, who had soldiered in Ireland, was chosen as governor of the colony, along with the scientist Thomas Hariot and the surveyor and artist John White, who was to bring back the first coloured sketches of life in North America. Raleigh was a thorough man and sent out the specialists necessary to plan and record the new-settled land of Virginia.

The fleet sailed in April 1585 – seven ships manned by 500 men, of which 108 were colonists. Prizes were sought and a fort built in Puerto Rico, where Grenville traded for livestock and stores for the colony. Then Grenville sailed his fleet up to Roanoke Island, where they were welcomed by the Indians. Grenville landed the colonists and their supplies and returned to England on the *Tiger*. Fortunately, he fell in with a Spanish cargo ship and captured it. When it was sold with its cargo in Plymouth, Raleigh and the Queen and the other patrons of the expedition were already in profit.

At Roanoke Island the colonists built a fort from a design by Hariot. The winter was mild and crops of maize were planted. Efforts to

grow sugarcane and wheat, oranges and lemons, failed. Yet Hariot learned of many local products: grass silk, worm silk, flax, hemp, alum, pitch, tar, sassafras, sweet gums, dyes such as sumac, okra, peas, gourds, and tobacco. The Indians constructed fish weirs for the colonists, taught them the medicinal properties of local herbs, and demonstrated how to extract flour from chestnuts. Without such lessons of how to live off the land, the Europeans could hardly have fed themselves. And with the discovery of the potato, parts of Europe itself would come to depend on the roots of America for survival, as well as for luxuries such as coffee, chocolate and vanilla.

In return, the colonists demonstrated their superior goods, particularly their iron weapons of war. Yet it was Hariot's scientific equipment that made the Indians believe the Europeans to be almost divine. He reported,

> Most things they saw with us, [such] as mathematical instruments, sea compasses, the virtue of the loadstone in drawing iron, a perspective

The arrival of the English at Roanoke, North Carolina, 1585.
From Thomas Hariot, A Brief and True Report . . . of Virginia, *1589.*

glass, whereby was showed many strange sights, burning glasses, wildfire works, guns, books (reading and writing), spring clocks that seem to go of themselves, and many other things that we had, were so strange unto them and so far exceeded their capacities to comprehend the reason and means how they should be made and done, that they thought they were rather the works of gods than of men.

The behaviour of the colonists soon persuaded the Indians that they were dealing with men. In the winter there were food shortages, and the colonists took what they were not given. The livestock ate the Indian plots of maize. The colonists seemed no longer gods or guests, but intruders and despoilers. The local Indian chief planned an attack with hundreds of men to destroy the colony. Instead, Ralph Lane and Hariot and some soldiers made a preventative attack on the chief's village and killed him and other Indians. While waiting for a counterassault, the colonists saw a fleet under Sir Francis Drake anchor off Roanoke Island after a successful raid on the Spanish

Indians eating a stew of fish and maize. Hariot, 1589.

Caribbean. The lack of a good harbour nearly sank Drake's ships in a June gale; but he remained long enough to embark Lane and the surviving colonists, who decided to abandon the fort and return home.

Soon after Drake had sailed away, a relief supply ship sent by Raleigh appeared at Roanoke Island. Finding no colonists there, it returned to England, as did Sir Richard Grenville's fleet, which also visited the place. Grenville left a token garrison of eighteen men to hold the fort, but after his departure, this small band had no chance against an Indian raid and was killed. The first American colony had ended in failure. It was undermanned and located in the wrong spot. Ralph Lane himself was not strong enough to endure. He did, however, reconnoitre Chesapeake Bay, where the colony should have been founded near a safe harbour.

Raleigh was not put out by the return of the first colonists. Immediately he began to plan a new expedition to set up a naval base in Chesapeake Bay. He would send out whole families, not men alone. Under the governorship of the experienced John White, they would settle and found a city in the New World. With his usual energy and sense of glory, Raleigh incorporated a City of Raleigh in Virginia with a coat of arms, a cross with the Raleigh roebuck in the top quarter of the shield. In April 1587 a flagship, the *Lion*, and two small vessels set sail from Plymouth, again piloted by Simon Fernandez. Once more the ships passed through the West Indies, then turned north to Roanoke Island, where the colonists were landed instead of in Chesapeake Bay. They renewed the abandoned fort and lived well on the easy gatherings of summer. Governor White himself decided to return to England and report to Raleigh and sail back with supply vessels. He left with Fernandez, while 114 colonists remained at Roanoke, two of them babies born in the New World.

White could not return. The following year was 1588, the year of the assault of the Spanish Armada on England. Ships and men could not be spared for the relief of a small colony overseas. A fleet assembled by Grenville was ordered to assist the Royal Navy, while a bark and a pinnace found by John White fell in with French privateers and were driven back to Plymouth.

In the absence of help, the colony was lost. Not until three years later did White return with a small fleet. He found an empty fort on Roanoke Island and a word burned into a wooden sign, CROATOAN, the name of a neighbouring island where the Indians under their

chief Manteo were still friendly to the English, who had instructed them. Losing contact with Europe, the colonists seem to have married into the local tribe. For the Croatoan Indians, who emigrated later to the interior of North Carolina, had fair-haired members in their group and used Elizabethan words in their language.

So the people of the New World checked and absorbed the advance body of the Old World. Raleigh himself lost thousands of pounds in the venture, but his choice of specialists led to the publishing of the first accurate information on 'Virginia'. John White's pictures and Thomas Hariot's *Brief and True Report of the New Found Land of Virginia* showed future promoters and colonists what to expect. Raleigh led the way for others to follow. His commitment was greater than his resources, his vision stronger than his powers. Yet he did cause a record to be made of the human beings, the creatures and the plants of the Atlantic coast of North America. He did instruct future settlers of the shape of things to come.

A Flying Fish.
John White, c. 1585.

A Flamingo.
John White.

An Iguana.
John White.

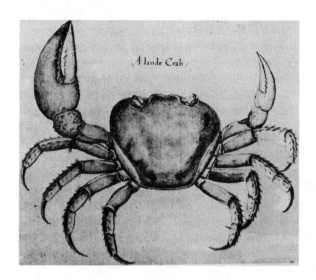

A Land Crab.
John White.

A Sea Turtle.
John White.

A Ritual Dance.
John White. By permission of the British Museum.

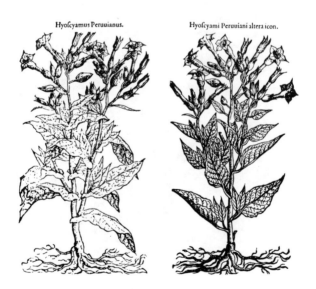

A Tobacco Plant.
From Rembert Dodoens, Stirpium Historiae Pemptades Sex., *1583.*

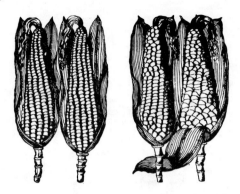

Maize.
From John Gerard, The Herbal or General History of Plants, *1597.*

A Potato Plant.
From a Flemish or German watercolour of 1588.
This is the first picture known of the potato.

RALEIGH, SPAIN AND RIVALRY

WHILE PLANTING HIS COLONIES IN North America, Raleigh did not stop sending out ships to raid in the Atlantic. One of these took an important prisoner, Don Pedro Sarmiento de Gamboa, the governor of the Straits of Magellan, the sea route to the Pacific. Sarmiento was well treated by Raleigh and introduced to the Queen and Lord Burghley. They wanted him released without payment of a ransom and sent to King Philip II of Spain on a peace mission. Raleigh consented. Sarmiento had told him of a fortune to be won. 'I had knowledge by relation,' Raleigh wrote, 'of that mighty, rich and beautiful Empire of Guiana, and of that great and golden city, which the Spaniards call El Dorado and the naturals Manoa.' In his turn, Raleigh told Sarmiento that he would represent Spanish interests in England for an annual pension in gold.

Sir John Hawkins had played the same game. He had taken a Spanish pension and had reported all that Spain wanted from him to the Privy Council. He had also not stopped from attacking Spain in the West Indies. King Philip II wisely declined Raleigh's offer of help, which was that of a double agent responsible primarily to England. Unfortunately, Raleigh's dealings with Spain through Sarmiento were to prove disastrous at his later trials for treason, when Queen Elizabeth was dead and King James on the throne.

Another mistake of Raleigh's which would do him future harm was his support of smoking tobacco. Thomas Hariot had praised its medicinal properties. It purged the evil humours of the body and prevented diseases. Raleigh himself tried to grow tobacco in Ireland and set the fashion for smoking a pipe at Court. He had a gold tobacco case set about with candles for lighting his pipe, and he even bet Queen Elizabeth that he could weigh the smoke. He did so by putting the pipe full of tobacco on the scales, then smoking it and weighing

it again filled with ash. The difference in ounces, he said, was the weight of the smoke. The Queen laughed and paid, joking that many men had turned gold into smoke, but he was the first to turn smoke into gold. He would not do that in his search for El Dorado.

He was no longer the Queen's only favourite. The young Robert Devereux, Earl of Essex, had won a knighthood fighting with his stepfather the Earl of Leicester in the Netherlands. He was chosen by the Queen to be her companion, although he was extravagant, reckless, spoiled and headstrong. He called Raleigh a wretch and a knave in the presence of the Queen and her Captain of the Guard. The Queen defended Raleigh, but soon promoted Essex to be her Master of the Horse and a Knight of the Garter.

Robert Devereux, Earl of Essex. From an engraving by Robert Boissard.

The Queen had need of her defenders. In 1587 she had allowed the execution of Mary Queen of Scots and had loosed Drake and the English fleet on Cadiz, where he sank so much Spanish shipping that the Catholic Armada could not sail that year. The following year, 130 ships left Spain to seize a Channel port and ferry across Spanish veterans from the Netherlands for the conquest of England. Raleigh himself was not allowed to serve on the flagship of the English fleet, the *Ark Royal*. He was ordered to defend Devon and Cornwall with the new troops of horsemen and infantry that he had raised in case of an invasion.

After the Armada had sailed past the West Country, Raleigh rode to London. The Queen was not pleased with the running battle along the Channel and the sending of fireships to scatter the Spanish fleet. The galleons were not being sunk or captured. She sent Raleigh to demand an assault on the Armada. The Royal Navy attacked, using all its munitions to kill thousands of Spanish sailors and soldiers and to cripple many of the galleons. Then the storms blew and the damaged Armada was driven north. Only half the ships survived, rounding Scotland and sailing back home.

Although Queen Elizabeth gave thanks to God for the storms that destroyed the Armada, Raleigh knew that the victory was the result of English strategy. He did not believe in tangling with the huge floating barracks of Spain. 'There is a great deal of difference in fighting loose, or at large,' he wrote, 'and grappling. The guns of a slow ship pierce as well, and make as great holes, as those in a swift.' Two of the vessels he had built, the *Ark Royal* and the *Roebuck*, fought well; they were both heavily armed and swift. They would always hurt the Spanish fleet at long range. 'To clap ships together without consideration, belongs rather to a madman than to a man of war.'

Grenville and Raleigh were ordered to prevent the Armada from landing in Ireland on its voyage back, but bad weather did their work for them. Raleigh himself was now interested in Ireland, for he had planted another colony there closer to home. As another mark of her favour and belief in him, the Queen had granted Raleigh control over 12,000 acres of the confiscated Desmond estates in Waterford and Cork. Raleigh sent families from Devon and Cornwall to settle there. His neighbours at home, however, proved bad tenants across the sea, and Irish hostility prevented good farming. The planting of potatoes flourished, but the cultivation of tobacco was unsuccessful. Irish

*A portrait of Queen Elizabeth, about 1590. She has her hand on
the globe and the ocean, while the victorious Royal Navy sails beside her.*

weather, as usual, proved stronger than experiments to change the face of the island.

Raleigh himself probably accompanied his ships on loan to the Royal Navy in the English counterattack on Spain of 1589. A large fleet and a small army assaulted Portugal in an effort to put a Portuguese Pretender on the throne, now linked with Spain. Essex's recklessness on land was useless, as the Portuguese fear of Spanish reprisals was greater than their desire to support a king of their own. The army was withdrawn, although Drake burned Vigo and 200 ships on the Tagus. Raleigh quarrelled with one of Essex's captains over prize money; he had already been prevented by the Privy Council from fighting a duel with his rival, Essex. The feud between them at Court was embarrassing the Queen, particularly as Leicester had died, leaving Essex as his heir to the Queen's old affections. Raleigh decided on a tactical retreat to his new estates, and the Queen did not forbid him to go. My Lord of Essex had chased Mr Raleigh from Court, one of the earl's supporters boasted, and had confined him to Ireland.

With his usual energy, Raleigh turned his confinement into an enterprise. He began the restoration of Lismore Castle as a home for himself and as a defence of the Queen's interests. He brought in miners to look for metals; they found coal instead. And he devoted himself to learning and historical studies and writing poetry, fired by his frequent meetings with his neighbour Edmund Spenser, the author of *The Faerie Queene*.

Writing fine poetry to Queen Elizabeth was a sure way to gain her favour. Leicester had been Spenser's patron; now Raleigh took on the role and decided to emulate the other poet, himself starting a long poem to Queen Elizabeth as Cynthia. Much of the poem is lost, but some of it survives in manuscript, particularly on Raleigh's feelings about being sent away from Court.

> His song was all a lamentable lay
> Of great unkindness and of usage hard,
> Of Cynthia, the Lady of the Sea,
> Which from her presence faultless him debarred . . .
>
> 'Ah, my love's queen and goddess of my life!
> Who shall me pity, where thou dost me wrong?'

Yet Raleigh did not blame the Queen so much as his rivals at Court and Court life itself. There was a love of truth and hatred of hypocrisy

in Raleigh that led him to strike out against the falsity of institutions and those who ran them. In his most angry – and modern – poem he attacked all those who attacked him.

> Say to the Court it glows
>   And shines like rotten wood,
> Say to the Church it shows
>   What's good, and doth no good.
> If Church and Court reply,
>   Then give them both the lie.

Such a powerful verse gave great offence. To denounce Church and Court was to invite denunciation. There were accusations that Raleigh was an atheist; if proved, it would have meant his execution. The charges were untrue, as Raleigh certainly believed in God and in the Church of England. 'He was scandalized with atheism,' John Aubrey revealed, 'but he was a bold man, and would venture at discourse which was unpleasant to the Churchmen.' His friends, however, included the playwright Christopher Marlowe, who died suddenly before his own trial for atheism; Thomas Hariot and John Dee, whose researches in science and astronomy and astrology laid them open to slander about their religious faith; and other free-thinking friends who were satirized by Shakespeare in *Love's Labour's Lost* as a 'School of Night'. As for the Court, Raleigh could defend himself well enough when he was there, as long as he retained royal favour. If he lost that, he might risk the fate of other fallen royal favourites. As a courtier wrote against Raleigh's poem on giving all the lie:

> Such is the song, such is the author
> Worthy to be rewarded with a halter.

Yet Raleigh's boldness and poetry pleased the Queen. He returned from Ireland to profit from the disgrace of Essex, who married Frances Walsingham, the widow of Sir Philip Sidney, fallen on the battlefield where Essex had been knighted. The Queen was jealous and unforgiving, and banished Essex to the country. She restored her faithful 'Water' Raleigh to his position near to her, although Essex was soon sent abroad as a Lord General to command English forces aiding the new Huguenot King of France, Henry of Navarre. Raleigh was appointed Vice-Admiral of a fleet to be sent to the Azores to capture the Spanish silver convoy; but at the last moment, the Queen again

decided that he must stay with her. Sir Richard Grenville took his cousin's place. His ship, victualled by Raleigh, was the *Revenge*.

Philip of Spain had been building new galleons, partially designed after the English model. Some of the new ships, including the *St Philip* and *St Andrew*, joined a powerful fleet ordered to attack the raiders. The English ships were caught at anchor. They had to hoist sail and try to escape. All succeeded except for Grenville on the *Revenge*. With half his men sick, surrounded by a whole enemy fleet, he decided to fight it out, not to try and flee. 'Out of the greatness of his mind,' Raleigh wrote of his cousin's decision, 'he could not be persuaded.' Grenville had always been a stubborn and headstrong man. Nothing brought him more honour than his going down.

The *Revenge* defended herself against galleon after galleon for fifteen hours, repelling endless boarding parties. She was bombarded into a hulk, holed by 800 shot, mastless, wallowing. Half her men were killed, most of the rest of the crew badly wounded, including Grenville. Two galleons were sunk, many others damaged, 1000 Spaniards dead. Grenville wanted the last of the gunpowder used to 'split and sink the ship', but his men would not do it. The survivors and the ship were taken, Grenville died of his wounds, and the *Revenge* and fifteen Spanish ships sank in a storm. The taking of the *Revenge*, a Dutch observer noted, was justly revenged upon the Spaniards, 'and not by the might or force of man, but by the power of God'.

Raleigh wrote an anonymous pamphlet, making a hero out of his cousin and creating a myth of courage for the Royal Navy. He turned a defeat into a victory, an error into a glory. He used the lost sea battle to attack Spanish greed and ambition. He had become Spain's chief enemy at Court. The Queen rewarded him once more with a rich estate at Sherborne in Dorset, where Raleigh was to make his home in the country.

He had need to prepare for a longer banishment. He wished to marry. He had always been attractive to women. The recent discovery of his will shows that he reputedly had a daughter with Alice Goold, probably from the West Country. The gossip John Aubrey tells a hilarious story of Raleigh making love to one of the Queen's Maids of Honour, whose protests of 'Nay, sweet Sir Walter! Sir Walter!' changed with the danger and the pleasure into cries of ecstasy, 'Swisser Swatter Swisser Swatter.' Unfortunately, Raleigh now com-

Sir Richard Grenville. By permission of the National Portrait Gallery.

mitted Essex's mistake with another of the Queen's Maids of Honour, Elizabeth Throckmorton, a beauty with slanting eyes under her high forehead and, as Raleigh wrote, 'a violet breath and lips of jelly'. He conceived a child with her and married her in secret, not daring to inform the Queen.

He knew that the Queen would punish him for the double blow of his faithlessness to her and her betrayal by one of her Maids of Honour. He sought to find a way to placate her by seizing the whole Spanish silver fleet and presenting it to her. He insisted on commanding the expedition, and the Queen consented, only to replace him with Sir Martin Frobisher. Raleigh still set sail with the raiding fleet, declaring to Lord Burghley's son, Sir Robert Cecil, that he was not married. 'For I protest before God, there is no one on the face of the earth that I would be fastened unto.' Yet his secret wife would soon give birth to his son Damerei, put him out to nurse, and return to Court as a Maid of Honour.

The expedition against the Spanish treasure convoy failed, as King Philip postponed its departure from the Americas. Raleigh split his ships into two raiding squadrons, sending them to look for prizes from the East Indies. He returned and waited for his fate in Durham House. The Queen would not see him, and he and his wife would not tell the Queen of the truth or of the child. It was thought, one courtier wrote, that Raleigh would lose all his places and preferments with the Queen's favour. 'Now he must fall as low as he was high, at the which many will rejoice.' Suddenly, the Queen acted and ordered Raleigh and his wife to be confined in the Tower of London. She would not be deceived by her Captain of the Guard and her Maid of Honour.

Once inside the Tower, Raleigh knew that the only key to unlocking the prison door was the Queen's forgiveness. So he wrote to her adviser, Sir Robert Cecil, in the poetic style that he knew might please the Queen. He told of his broken heart now that the Queen had left him for country life in the summer. She was far away, riding like Alexander, hunting like Diana, and walking like Venus, while he was 'in a dark prison, all alone'. He claimed to be more weary of life than his enemies were desirous to take it from him. He would be happy to die for his Queen or by her side. He was unworthy of any name or title. He signed himself plain W.R.

Yet Raleigh hoped for quick forgiveness after the Queen had made

an example of him. Judging by her treatment of Essex, he need not expect to stay in the Tower for long. He was correct. The Queen soon discovered that she needed him again for his authority, for his energy, and for his loyalty to her.

V

THE LIBERTY OF THE COUNTRY

RALEIGH'S PLANNING HAD MADE his sea expedition finally profitable. One of his squadrons had fallen in with the huge Portuguese carrack, the *Mother of God*, loaded with jewels, spices, carpets, ivory, drugs and silks. It was the richest prize ever captured by the Elizabethans at sea. When it was sailed back to Dartmouth, there was an orgy of pillaging and looting. The excuse for some of the plundering was the imprisonment of Raleigh, the leader of the West Country as well as of the expedition. The Queen's share was in jeopardy. She ordered Raleigh to be released from the Tower so that he could hasten to Devon and restore order. Raleigh, as Sir John Hawkins pointed out, was 'the especial man'.

Raleigh needed to protect his own share as well as the Queen's. He received a tumultuous welcome. 'His poor servants, to the number of a hundred and forty goodly men,' Sir Robert Cecil reported, 'and all the mariners, came to him with such shouts and joy, as I never saw a man more troubled to quiet them in my life.' Raleigh laboured to recover the looted spoils and made an unfair division of them, giving the Queen the lion's share and himself the least. When congratulated on being free, he replied that he was still the Queen's captive. And the Queen, not impressed by his generosity, put him back in the Tower with his wife. They were both released in December and banished from the Queen's presence to freedom at Sherborne.

Calculation and statecraft governed the Queen's rage against her favourite. Raleigh was a leader in the West Country. The Queen had made him so. She needed his authority in her name and his support. There had been a Catholic rebellion in Devon when she had been young. Raleigh and his many kinsmen and supporters had been able to raise ships and crews, horsemen and soldiers at the time of the Armada. If she kept Raleigh in the Tower too long, she might risk a rising against herself.

Raleigh was loyal, however, and he knew that the customs of feudal times only lingered. The throne was growing stronger. This was the last reign in which the Crown could call upon the aristocracy and the gentry to raise large numbers of troops for national service. Even in the West Country, sailors had to be pressganged to serve in the Royal Navy or on raids against Spain. Raleigh had personal power and authority, but it was diminishing with the years. As he wrote during the reign of Queen Elizabeth's successor, 'There were many earls could bring into the field a thousand barbed horses, many a baron five or six hundred barbed horses, whereas now very few of them can furnish twenty to serve the King.' It was the same with munitions of war. 'The noblemen had in their armories to furnish some of them a thousand, some two thousand, some three thousand men, whereas now there are not many that can arm fifty.'

It was not so at sea. Private shipbuilders such as Raleigh contributed the bulk of the English navy, although the royal ships usually led in

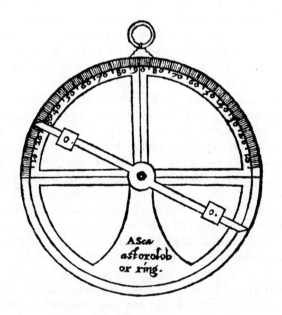

An improved astrolabe or mariner's ring.
From William Bourne, A Regiment for the Sea, *1576.*

design and firepower. In the countryside at Sherborne, Raleigh could concentrate on his many interests, particularly on naval improvements, science, chemistry and better agriculture. His patronage of the researches of Thomas Hariot and John Dee, and his insistence that his sea captains learned navigation as well as practical seamanship had contributed to the rise of English naval power.

During the forty years of Raleigh's life, there had been a sea-change in the English contribution to the Age of Discovery. Pilots and instruments from the Mediterranean countries were no longer needed to guide English ships to far continents. As John Davis stated in his significant manual of 1594, *The Seamans Secrets*, Englishmen were no longer pupils. They were second to none as navigators or practical seamen. Many hundreds were as competent as himself on the oceans. They had learned from their scientists and their astronomers and their map-makers as well as from the long voyages of exploration. By improved sea-compasses and cross-staffs, quadrants and astrolabes,

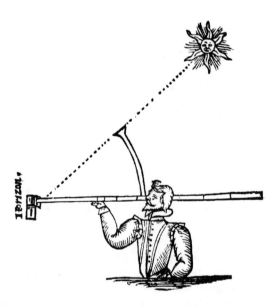

An improved cross-staff, renamed a back-staff, used for solar observations, 1594.
From John Davis, The Seamans Secrets.

charts and globes, English mariners could steer their own course. They had profited from the few enlightened patrons such as Raleigh, who had promoted scientific advances as well as colonial ventures.

Raleigh's experiments in chemistry and medicine were many, but obscure. John Aubrey thought him a great chemist with a particularly good cure for fever. His spirit of bold, persistent enquiry led him to try and try again to understand the matter of nature and the universe. Searching for everything from the philosopher's stone that would turn base metal into gold to a better way of breeding falcons, he invited his free-thinking friends of the 'School of Night' to test theory and practice in long disputations. His thrusting mind that challenged traditions and beliefs unsettled his conservative neighbours. There was even a three-day hearing at Cerne Abbas to investigate Raleigh's religious creed. He was acquitted of any charge of heresy or atheism.

Instead of living in the old castle at Sherborne, Raleigh began to build a manor house in the shape of a brick pepperpot, sprouting tall chimneys and stone roebucks. He laid out gardens and made a park round ornamental water. His son Damerei died, but his wife bore him another son, named Walter or 'Wat' after his father. He bred racehorses and birds of prey, and he planted trees and crops. He even developed a timber business in barrel staves from his Irish estates, but they did not prosper in his absence.

Raleigh only travelled to London to serve as a Member of Parliament. His independent thinking and speaking made their mark in the House of Commons. He spoke up for subsidies and for the exclusion of foreign goods from the English market. He urged open war with Spain. But his most telling speeches were in defence of religious freedom. He opposed a bill condemning an extreme Puritan sect, the Brownists, who wished to separate from the Church of England. Although the Queen herself as head of the Anglican Church equated religious dissent with treason, Raleigh defended freedom of worship. To him, conscience was its own law and beyond the law.

Such outspoken views in Parliament made Raleigh a hero to the Puritan opposition. He seemed ready to defy Court and official policy, although he always protested his loyalty to the Queen. She remained aloof, taking her counsel from the old Lord Burghley, from his son Sir Robert Cecil, and from Essex, now restored to favour. Even Raleigh's ally, the Earl of Northumberland, found his friend's behaviour

provocative. 'I know him insolent,' he wrote, 'extremely heated, a man that desires to seem to be able to sway all men's courses.'

This energy, this power of leadership, led Raleigh to leave his country life and reach out for a quest that might bring him back to England a conqueror with riches greater than avarice might imagine. He resolved to lead an expedition in search of El Dorado, the fabled golden city of Guiana.

VI

THE QUEST FOR EL DORADO

WHEN THE SPANIARDS SEIZED rooms full of gold ornaments from the Incas, they never found the mines from which the metal came. Gonzalo Jiménez de Quesada set off with an expedition to find the mines in the Amazonian jungles; most of his men died, including his brother, struck by a bolt of lightning; he survived to pass on his quest to Lope de Aguirre. Aguirre and his men did discover the connection between the Amazon and the Orinoco Rivers, the Rio Negro, before he was beheaded for treason. They both believed in the legend of a golden city named El Dorado, where the emperor was so rich that he used gold dust as powder on his body.

Quesada bequeathed the search for El Dorado to his heir Antonio de Berrio, who set up a base on the island of Trinidad at the mouth of the Orinoco. Berrio made three sorties into the interior as far as the mountains. He brought back geographical knowledge and news of gold mines. Raleigh knew of Berrio's endeavours from his captive Sarmiento. He wanted himself to find El Dorado and to establish a seaboard empire in Guiana after his failure in North Carolina. It was the only large area of tropical America not garrisoned by the Spanish or the Portuguese. Raleigh also saw gold itself not only as riches, but as the instrument of power. The Spanish King's Indian gold 'endangereth and disturbeth all the nations of Europe, it purchaseth intelligence, creepeth into Councils, and setteth bound loyalty at liberty, in the greatest Monarchies'.

Raleigh's wife did not want him to leave home and sail to the jungles and fevers of Guiana. Once he had begun raising funds and supporters and soldiers, ships and crews for his planned expedition, she wrote to Sir Robert Cecil, 'I hope you will rather draw Sir Walter towards the East, than help him forward towards the sunset . . . Stay him rather than further him, by the which you shall bind me for

The emperor of El Dorado being powdered with gold dust. From Theodore de Bry,
Americae Pars VIII . . ., *1599. By permission of the British Library.*

ever.' Yet no prohibition by an indifferent Queen or a cautious Cecil
stopped Raleigh from sending out a reconnaissance mission in 1594,
which brought back intelligence of how Berrio was hated by the
Indian tribes. The next year Raleigh sailed with 150 men other than
his sailors, four ships and a galley for rowing in shallow waters. He
had letters patent which allowed him to discover and possess all land
unpossessed by a Christian Prince, also to offend and enfeeble the
King of Spain.

When Raleigh's ships reached Trinidad, he surprised Berrio and
his small garrison in the newly built city of St Joseph. He made a
dawn attack on the city, burning it and slaughtering its inhabitants.
Berrio was taken prisoner and treated as well as Sarmiento had
been. Raleigh needed all of Berrio's information about the route
to El Dorado, and Berrio fed his captor's dreams of the fabled city,

Raleigh burns St Joseph in Trinidad and captures Berrio, 1595.
From Theodore de Bry, Americae Pars VIII . . ., *1599.*

placing it on a mountain lake between the Orinoco and the Amazon.

If Raleigh was ruthless in refusing the risk of a Spanish force at his back, he was considerate in his policy towards the Indians. He freed five native chiefs, who had been chained and tortured by Berrio. They were only too glad to follow their liberator, who promised to protect them against the Spaniards. Raleigh's treatment of the Indians was enlightened, because he knew he would depend on them if he wished to maintain an empire in Guiana against a Spanish counterattack. He set out four points to be followed: the Indians must always be defended against the Spaniards, they must be aided to recover their territory as far as Peru, they must be instructed in civil and social behaviour, and they must be taught how to use European weapons. It was a wise and far-seeing policy to win the hearts and minds of the original Americans.

After securing his rear, Raleigh threaded his way through the skein

The city of Manoa or El Dorado on its lake in the mountains.
From L. Hulsius, Travels . . ., *1599.*

of rivers in the Orinoco delta. With him went 100 men and Lawrence Keymis, another Hariot, an Oxford mathematician and geographer and mariner. They progressed on the galley and four ship's boats into the little-known country 'that hath yet her maidenhead'. There, Raleigh wrote, 'The face of the earth hath not been torn, nor the virtue and salt of the soil spent.'

Winds helped their small sails as far as the cataracts. Then they had to carry the boats past the white waters dashing against the rocks. Upriver, the currents flowed fiercely. It was slow rowing all the way. The sun burned them, their supplies ran short. There were loud voices of dissent, but Raleigh persisted in case the world laughed them to scorn.

Raleigh saw his New World truly and through the spectacles of myth. There were bright red and crimson birds, also orange-tawny, purple and green. There were thousands of the ugly serpents called

*Raleigh welcomed by the Caique of the Arromaia Indians before receiving their
allegiance and putting them under the protection of Queen Elizabeth of England.
From Theodore de Bry,* Americae Pars VIII . . ., *1599.
By permission of the British Library.*

alligators, which ate one of his men. Yet Raleigh also claimed to hear
of ferocious Amazon women who killed all men they did not need to
procreate, and the headless Ewaipanoma with mouths in their chests
and eyes in their shoulders. With a suffering body and his head in
the clouds, Raleigh pressed on towards El Dorado.

The expedition reached the savannah of the uplands. Some Spanish
canoes were captured, full of baked bread and gold ore and a refiner's
outfit for assaying metal. An Indian guide was found so that the
English could visit all the river villages, where they were welcomed
and fed. They were careful to treat the Indians with courtesy and
leave their women alone. Their health was remarkable. Not an

A map of Guiana based on Raleigh's writings.
The fabulous Ewaipanoma and Amazons are depicted.
From L. Hulsius, Travels . . ., 1599. By permission of the British Library.

Englishman fell ill, although Raleigh was shown the remedy against
the prick of poisoned arrows, the tupara root, and made it and
quinine the base of his medicines against fevers. He granted Queen
Elizabeth's protection to Topiawari, the aged chief of the savannah
country, who confirmed the existence of the mountain lake of El
Dorado with its great city on its shores and waters filled with golden
tributes. On the far horizon, Raleigh could see the twin peaks the
Indians called Picatoa and Inatac, the gateway to El Dorado.

   Yet he could not reach there. The rainy season was beginning, the
rivers rising. Topiawari asked him to return with an army the
following year; then they would attain El Dorado. Raleigh left two

Raleigh's march to the interior of Guiana with Indian porters.
In the background, the mountains reputed to hold the lake of El Dorado.
From Theodore de Bry, Americae Pars VIII . . ., *1599.*

Englishmen behind as a pledge for his return and for two of
Topiawari's sons that were to go back to Europe. Then he and his
men left downriver for the sea. Raleigh created an enchanted land
from the savannah, describing it as the most beautiful country he had
ever seen: 'Hills raised here and there, over the valleys, the river
winding into different branches, plains without bush or stubble, all
fair green grass, deer crossing our path, the birds toward evening
singing on every side a thousand different tunes, herons of white,

crimson, and carnation perching on the river-side, the air fresh with a gentle wind.'

His description was a brochure, a promotion for an empire in Guiana that Raleigh had not yet won. He was returning without profit or gold. He sent off Lawrence Keymis and some men in search of a reported gold mine. Keymis returned with samples of ore said to be gold and hacked from a cliff; but there was no proof positive. Raleigh plundered two Spanish settlements on the voyage home, but an attack on a third was beaten off with heavy loss, and he had to give up his captive Berrio, his witness of the truth of El Dorado. So he returned to ridicule in England, a knight errant in search of fool's gold.

There were those who declared that even the ore Raleigh had found bore no gold. There were those who insinuated that he had been paid by Spain to accomplish nothing. There were those who said that he had never left Cornwall, but had taken his backers' money for himself. In a fury, Raleigh wrote of his travels and adventures, *The Discovery of the Large, Rich, and Beautiful Empire of Guiana, with a Relation of the Great and Golden City of Manoa*. Raleigh had only penetrated 200 miles inland, but he made it appear that he had found an empire ready for the taking. His mixture, however, of true observation and traveller's tale, of history and fable, of lure and strategy of empire, made him seem both inspiring and credulous, a figure of the Age of Dream as well as of Discovery. As in the colonizing of 'Virginia', his ambitions were greater than his means, his visions ranged further than the capacity of his Queen to support them.

The publication of the *Discovery* elevated Raleigh into a man of myth himself, daring, legendary, incredible. He had added to the English Crown the title of the Empress of Guiana and El Dorado. He had claimed that 'whatsoever Prince shall possess it shall be greatest; and if the King of Spain enjoy it, he will become unresistible'. But the Queen did not seize the opportunity, nor did she believe the source. Instead, she sent Raleigh and her captains to resist the King of Spain in his own land.

VII

COUNTERATTACK ON SPAIN

Raleigh's expedition to Guiana told hard on him. He returned, he said, a withered beggar: although he was only forty-three years old, already he was 'in the winter of his life'. Yet his commitment to an empire in the Caribbean made him throw himself into another attack on Spain. Fear that a new armada was being prepared to invade Ireland and England led Queen Elizabeth to license a massive raid on the Spanish coast. Drake and Hawkins had died of illness on a last voyage to the West Indies, but the Queen still had captains enough to show her power on the sea.

Raleigh was recalled to command one of the four squadrons of the large English fleet of nearly 100 ships, supported by twenty-four small Dutch vessels. The other commanders were the Earl of Essex, Lord Admiral Charles Howard and Lord Thomas Howard. Sir Francis Vere was to lead an invasion force of 10,000. Raleigh was given the forty-gun royal vessel, the *Warspite*, as his flagship. He found it difficult to pay for stores and press seamen to serve. Time dragged by and winds were contrary. 'Sir, by the living God,' he protested to Cecil, 'there is no King nor Queen nor general nor any else can take more care than I do to be gone.'

Finally, in June 1596, the English fleet set sail for the great Spanish port of Cadiz. Their leaders were already falling out with one another, each wanting pride of place; but fair winds took them quickly to their destination. On its spit of land, Cadiz defended the narrow neck of water leading to the fifty merchantmen from the West Indies that sheltered in its bay. Fortresses and batteries dominated the entrance, which was blocked by the great galleons called the 'Four Apostles', two of which had captured the *Revenge*. In support were three frigates and twenty galleys.

Raleigh was not present at the final conference that decided the

Detail from 'Carta Atlantica', 1525.
By permission of the Bibliothèque Nationale, Paris
(Départment des Cartes et Plans).

Queen Elizabeth I, c. 1575, attributed to Nicholas Hilliard.
By permission of the National Portrait Gallery.

Sir Walter Raleigh, *c. 1585.*
Miniature by Nicholas Hilliard.
By permission of
the National Portrait Gallery.

Sir Francis Drake, *c. 1581.*
Miniature by Nicholas Hilliard.
By permission of
the National Portrait Gallery.

Map of the American coastline from Florida to the Chesapeake by John White.
By permission of the British Museum Library.

Indian in body paint by John White.
By permission of the British Museum Library.

The Indian village of Secotan by John White.
By permission of the British Museum Library.

Sir Walter Raleigh and his son, 1602, by an unknown artist.
By permission of the National Portrait Gallery.

Royal procession to mark the marriage of a Maid of Honour, 1600,
by Marcus Gheeraerts the Younger.
By permission of Colonel Wingfield-Digby, Sherborne Castle.

King James I, by an unknown artist,
after J. de Critz the Elder.
*By permission of
the National Portrait Gallery.*

Somerset House Conference of 1604, by an unknown Flemish artist.
By permission of the National Portrait Gallery

The Boyhood of Raleigh, by Sir John Millais.
By permission of the Tate Gallery.

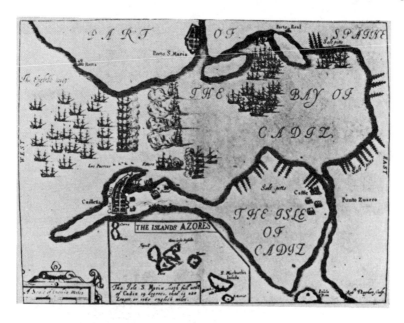

The English fleet attacks the Spanish galleons blocking the Bay of Cadiz, 1596.
From a contemporary engraving.

English plan of battle. It was not a good plan. Essex was to land and attack Cadiz from within its walls. Nothing was to be done to assault the galleons and force the entrance to the bay. Bad weather aborted the plan. Two of the landing craft capsized. Raleigh returned and persuaded Essex to back his idea of an immediate assault on Cadiz Bay, thrusting through the narrow channel between the fortresses. He then persuaded the Lord Admiral to support his new tactics. He was to lead the assault in the *Warspite*. He had effectively taken over the command by his daring and his resolution.

At dawn, Raleigh sailed against the Four Apostles and the twenty galleys that waited, ready to ram and sink the invaders. He had resolved 'to be revenged for the *Revenge*' or to second his cousin Grenville's death with his own life. The *Warspite*'s guns soon sent the 'wasps' of the galleys buzzing away; but Raleigh's vessel was bombarded by the improved cannon of the Four Apostles. There was

no room for manoeuvre, so that Raleigh had to discard his usual strategy of pounding the Spanish galleons at long range, while avoiding their gunshots.

Moreover, the other English captains and officers were forcing their ships forward. Sir Francis Vere's *Rainbow* and the *Nonpareil* of the Lords Howard were pushing past the *Warspite* to be first into action. Raleigh edged his ship past the *Rainbow*, only to find that Vere threw a cable aboard to pull his ship nearer to the fight. Raleigh cut the cable and steered straight at the *St Philip* and grappled with her.

The *Warspite* was riddled with Spanish cannon balls, but the fierceness of the English onslaught made the Spaniards panic. They cut their mooring cables. The galleons were wrecked on shore, where they were set on fire. The thousands of soldiers aboard fell into the sea and were slaughtered by the English ships, coming in for the kill. Raleigh himself was wounded by a cannon ball, which drove splinters from the deck into his leg. So he lay on the *Warspite*, watching the Spanish troops burn or drown or suffocate in the mud, 'so thick as if coals had been poured out of a sack'.

Essex and Vere landed with the English soldiers and sacked Cadiz. The fifty merchantmen in the bay were ignored, while the city was looted, then held to ransom. So the greatest prize was lost. The wounded Raleigh wanted to seize the merchant ships, then negotiate a huge penalty for their release. His advice was set aside. While the English commanders bartered for the ransom of Cadiz, all the merchant fleet was set on fire to keep it from being captured. Booty worth two million ducats to redeem was lost while haggling for a tenth of that. Drake's old plan for fortifying and holding Cadiz was abandoned. The English soldiers were embarked, and the squadrons sailed away. Another town was sacked, a bishop's library taken to form the basis for the new Bodleian Library at Oxford, but little else was achieved. The Howards and Raleigh turned down Essex's wish to cruise off the Azores and intercept the silver fleet from the Americas. A victory had been won, English sea power had been proved, even if a golden opportunity had been lost.

The Queen was not pleased. The spoils were too small to pay for her investment in the expedition. Yet the English people were proud of the humiliation of Spain. Essex took for himself most of the credit for the storming of Cadiz; the services of the other commanders were discounted. Essex, however, recognized the value of Raleigh's advice and example. Briefly, the two rivals showed good feelings towards

each other. Raleigh also used Sir Robert Cecil's friendship to gain the Queen's favour again. He needed to return to Court.

For five years the Queen had kept him in disgrace and in exile in the country, although she had not appointed another Captain of the Guard. Now she forgave him and restored him to his place close to her person, if not to her heart. He swore in new members of her Guard and stayed beside Her Majesty. 'Now he comes boldly to the privy chamber,' a courtier noted. It was as he used to do, only he limped from his wound at Cadiz. He had never been, he admitted, a footman. He would now find standing by the Queen or marching to war most hard for the rest of his years.

King Philip of Spain was bound to retaliate for the destruction of his great naval base. He ordered another armada to be prepared. He wanted to strike at England through Ireland, where Catholic rebels were still fighting the Protestant English colonists planted by Raleigh and other Elizabethan landowners.

Sir Robert Cecil had become the Queen's Principal Secretary as his father was dying. The Queen called her hunchbacked adviser her 'pygmy', but he was a giant in his overwork and his manipulation of others in his own and the royal interest. Although cautious by nature, he supported another attack on Spain to be led by Essex and Raleigh. It might prevent the sailing of a new armada and would put Cecil's two Court rivals out at sea and in danger. Cecil had reconciled them and was their apparent friend. Yet he wanted also to be the Queen's sole adviser and support. 'If we lived not in a cunning world,' Essex's uncle warned his nephew, 'I should assure myself that Mr Secretary were wholly yours.'

Another large English fleet was assembled. The plan was to attack the northern Spanish port of Ferrol, where the new Spanish armada was being outfitted. The silver convoy from the Americas was also to be intercepted. But July gales wrecked the expedition. Raleigh on the *Warspite* was battered in the Bay of Biscay and driven back to Plymouth with broken bulkheads and splintered sides. Essex's ship was sinking as it was blown back to its home port. God had turned the heavens against them, Raleigh informed Cecil. It was beyond the power or will of man to resist. Lord Thomas Howard did reach the Spanish coast, but without support he had to return and collect the rest of the fleet.

A fresh strategy was devised. The Queen still wanted an attack on the Spanish armada with fireships, while Raleigh supported Essex in

planning a naval expedition to the Azores where the annual silver convoy could be taken. More stormy weather drove the English ships away from any attempt against Ferrol. The squadrons were separated. Essex reached the Azores ten days before Raleigh joined him with his vessels. Already Essex's supporters had convinced him that Raleigh meant to desert him and ambush the treasure fleet on his own. Essex protested that he had never believed Raleigh would not join him, but he protested too much. While Raleigh was supplying and watering his ships, Essex and Lord Thomas Howard set off for the island of Fayal, ordering Raleigh to follow. But when Raleigh arrived there, the main English fleet was nowhere to be seen. It had gone to set a trap for the silver convoy without Raleigh.

Now the Spanish forts on Fayal opened fire on the *Warspite* and its supporting vessels. Raleigh refused to counterattack. Essex was officially his superior officer and would resent independent action from Raleigh. For four days, nothing was done. At a Council of War, those of Essex's captains with Raleigh refused to assault Fayal until their commander returned. Raleigh insisted on sending a party to land in search of water, even without the support of Essex's ships.

The watering party came under musket fire from the enemy. Raleigh immediately decided to attack. With 260 men he landed on the beach, losing some of the ship's boats on the rocks. He routed a Spanish force of 500 and sent them fleeing from their trenches. Giving them no time to recover, he advanced with his men on the town four miles away. He seemed indifferent to danger, wearing a white scarf and no armour. Limping, he led his troops to assault the first of the two forts defending the town. When fierce fire pinned them down, Raleigh insisted on pressing forward to reconnoitre. He put his armour on, but his white scarf still made him a mark for the Spanish shot that grazed him in several places. His courage and advance broke the nerve of the enemy. The Spaniards abandoned the fort and the town, taking refuge in the second citadel and the mountains of the interior.

Now Essex and Howard returned with their ships. They had failed to find the treasure fleet. Instead, they found Raleigh gaining glory from the attack on Fayal. Essex was advised to court-martial Raleigh and execute him for refusing to obey orders. But Raleigh, informed of Essex's coming, was rowed out to meet his rival. He expected praise for initiative, not blame and a death sentence.

An Elizabethan gunner firing a siege cannon, 1590.
From Webbe, His Travails . . .

Essex accused him of insubordination, but Raleigh defended his actions. He was a Rear-Admiral commissioned directly by the Queen. In the absence of Essex and Howard, he had to take decisions on his own. Essex was not appeased. Even if Raleigh's reasoning was sound, he had offended Essex's pride and position. At this moment, Lord Thomas Howard became the conciliator. He persuaded Raleigh to accept a censure from Essex and to apologize for his action. This gesture saved Essex's honour and Raleigh's neck. It did not help in subduing the garrison of Fayal.

Raleigh's impetuous assault, however, had been more successful than he knew. The second fort was abandoned overnight. There was no resistance to overcome. The town was burned, and the English fleet set sail for the island of Terceira, where the strong defences of the port of Angra could provide an impregnable harbour for the silver convoy. Essex ordered his ships to block the sea entrance to Angra, then changed his mind. Leaving only four vessels behind, he sailed

with his fleet to patrol the eastern approaches. Three hours later, the silver convoy sailed in to Angra, brushing aside the few English ships at the harbour mouth.

Essex returned with the main fleet too late. He wanted to assault Angra, but Howard and Raleigh pointed out that the enterprise would fail. Angra was too heavily fortified and garrisoned. Essex then decided on a blockade. The English would seize another island in the Azores, St Michael, and use it as a base to catch the silver convoy on its homeward course to Spain. There was another catalogue of errors. Raleigh was made to pretend a dummy attack, while Essex failed to press the real assault in the rear. The young earl changed his mind as frequently as the wind and forgot to inform his other officers of the shift. A wealthy prize, an East Indian carrack, was also lost: prematurely attacked, its captain beached and burned it. The onset of October storms caused the lifting of the blockade and blew the English ships home, having achieved nothing.

In fact, their absence had nearly created a disaster. A fresh Spanish armada had sailed from Ferrol. The two fleets were navigating on parallel courses towards the coasts of England. Once back at Plymouth, Raleigh set about recruiting troops to secure the West Country, while Essex rode to London to organize its defence. The fiasco of the voyage to the Azores was forgotten during the national peril. Yet again the storms blew and scattered the new armada. England was saved once more by the weather.

The Queen was displeased. She began to see Essex's shortcomings as a commander on deck and in the field. His indecisive service at sea and his censure of Raleigh's initiative showed both vanity and weakness. His official report even omitted to mention the expedition's only success, Raleigh's capture of Fayal. And finally, the Queen's favour depended more on her favourite giving her good advice and being successful than on holding her affections. Essex began to lose his place at Court without knowing it, while Raleigh was waiting in the wings, unsure of any friend or of the royal favour. He knew courage and resolution were not enough. For luck and time changed all positions. As his bitter poem stated:

> Tell fortune of her blindness,
>   Tell nature of decay,
> Tell friendship of unkindness,
>   Tell justice of delay.

And if they will reply,
Then give them all the lie.

The thing was, to survive, to be loyal, to serve the Queen, and never to prefer oneself above her.

VIII

THE FALL OF THE RIVAL

RALEIGH KNEW HOW THE CROWN
had grown in power at the expense of the nobles, who no longer had
the followers or the arsenals to threaten the monarch. The Earl of
Essex seemed not to know. Only thirty-one years of age after his
failure in the Azores, he was ruining himself from his spending on
war, retainers and extravagant living. Queen Elizabeth might shower
him with parks and woods, estates and monopolies, but he overspent
his income on acquiring a private army of supporters and soldiers.
Heavily in debt to the London merchants and bankers, he depended
on the Queen's continuing favour. But when she began to withdraw
it, he realized that he could not go on living and acting like some
Prince Consort.

He also did not know something that Raleigh knew all too well. To
preserve her power, the Queen balanced her advisers one against
another, depending on their rivalry. Just as she had played the dying
Burghley against the dead Leicester, and later Essex against Raleigh,
so she now played Cecil and Charles Howard against Essex. She was
the Queen, she would be arbiter and judge. And when she heard of
Essex in his vainglory attracting round him a group of discontented
noblemen, she saw a danger to the Crown. She was more than twice
the age of Essex, declining in health and without a direct heir, except
perhaps for her relation, King James VI of Scotland. Essex, however,
had brought to his cause other thwarted young peers – Southampton,
Mounteagle, Bedford, Sussex and Rutland – along with the older
Lords Sandys and Cromwell. All were living beyond their income, all
were feeling excluded from the favours and patronage of the Queen,
who was becoming increasingly mean to all her courtiers in order to
scrape up enough money to pay for the costs of fighting the Irish
rebellion.

Without a seizure of power, without effectively making the Queen

Robert Devereux, Second Earl of Essex, c. 1597.
By Marcus Gheeraerts the Younger. By permission of the National Portrait Gallery.

their hostage, Essex and his group of peers could not gain the grant of more monopolies or estates. They were tired of being sent to fight in profitless Irish wars, where the Earl of Tyrone was now leading the rebels, ruining Raleigh's estates in Munster and causing their owner to try and divest himself of them. Raleigh himself no longer wanted to go and fight again in Ireland, even to salvage his land. But when, at a Privy Council meeting, his cousin Sir George Carew was proposed as commander of the English forces there rather than Essex's uncle, Essex lost his temper with the Queen, Cecil and Charles Howard, now created Earl of Nottingham. He glared at the Queen and turned his back on her. She slapped him and told him to go and be hanged. He put a hand on his sword and swore he would not tolerate such an insult, not even from King Henry VIII. Howard intervened to stop any more violence between the Queen and her favourite, who retired to sulk on his country estate.

Essex could not resist making a display of his might. Although warned not to provoke the Queen, he burst in on a royal tournament to celebrate the Queen's birthday at the head of 2,000 armed men, overwhelming Raleigh and the Queen's Guard in a show of gaudy power. Essex had insolently dressed his men in the orange-tawny of the Queen's Guard, forcing Her Majesty to see that he could afford a greater protection than she could – and that he could protect her or make her a prisoner without benefit of her aggrieved Captain of the Guard, Sir Walter Raleigh.

The solution to the problem of Essex seemed to be to send him and his retainers to Ireland, the graveyard of so much English military ambition. Accompanied by his circle of knights and supporters, he made a triumphant ride through the streets of London, cheered by the mob. He crossed the Irish Sea with the largest force ever sent there by Queen Elizabeth, 16,000 foot and 1,300 horsemen. Yet Essex dallied in Dublin and negotiated a truce with Tyrone. He would lose his reputation by futile campaigns in Celtic mists and bogs. He also appeared to be holding his army in reserve, not to attack rebels in Ireland, but to return as a rebel to England.

The Queen sent him letters, urging him to attack Tyrone. Fear was sweeping through her country in the August of 1599. Once again a Spanish armada had sailed. Raleigh was ordered to join Lord Thomas Howard in readying the Royal Navy for service against an enemy invasion. But who was the enemy? The Spanish fleet or the army in Ireland under Essex? (Two years later, Essex's man Sir Christopher

Blount confessed before his execution that his master had thought of landing in Wales and marching with his army on London.)

Whether the evidence was false or true, Essex decided to return with only a few men, deserting his command. He burst into the Queen's Bedchamber at Nonesuch, catching her in disarray. She was pleasant to him, apparently forgiving while she listened to the tale of his wrongs and woes. But he had left his post, disobeyed her orders and threatened the throne itself. He was put under arrest and brought before the full Privy Council. He was spared a trial for treason, but confined to his house under guard for a year.

There Essex began to reveal the madness of his suspicions. He saw Raleigh as the tool of a Spanish plot. His rival would hand over the English coastline to the armada while Cecil and Charles Howard subverted the Privy Council with Spanish gold. Essex saw himself and his supporters as the only true friends of the Queen and of her likely heir, King James VI of Scotland, who was warned by Essex of this imaginary plot. Essex wanted the Scottish King to intervene by force to protect his right to the English throne. The King, however, sent an embassy south, not an army. By the time it arrived in London, Essex had carried out his own plot against the Queen and her advisers.

Knowing Essex as his enemy and seeing the danger to the Crown, Raleigh recommended to Cecil that Essex should be detained for life. Wisdom demanded the elimination of all risk from him. 'If you take it for a good counsel to relent towards this tyrant,' Raleigh wrote, 'you will repent it when it shall be too late. His malice is fixed, and will not evaporate.' The less made of Essex, the less he could cause harm. If the Queen spurned him, he would decline to a common person. And he would always be a threat to the Queen's safety. 'I have seen the last of her good days, and all ours, after his liberty.'

Cecil was wilier than Raleigh. He believed that the headstrong Essex, set at liberty, would condemn himself. Cecil applied his policy, persuading the Queen to free the young earl. He had menaced her, writing that he would 'come in armour, triumphing' into her presence. Raleigh even maintained that Essex jeered at the Queen, saying that her conditions were as crooked as her carcass. Such a remark would never be forgiven.

Essex now plotted to seize power. He corresponded with Mountjoy, who had taken over command of the army in Ireland, but refused to invade England with it. Essex House in London became a meeting

place for all the opposition, from poor noblemen to Puritan radicals. A date for a rebellion was set. Shakespeare's company of actors was hired to present in a theatre a performance of *Richard the Second*, a play in which an evil king was rightly overthrown. History was the drama of present life.

An Elizabethan theatre, the Swan, 1596. From a drawing by John de Witt.

Knowing of the conspiracy, Raleigh increased the guard round the Queen. He sent for his cousin, Sir Ferdinando Gorges, who was a supporter of Essex. They met in the middle of the Thames near Essex House, each in a rowing boat. Raleigh ordered Gorges to rejoin the Queen's service, while Gorges assured Raleigh that he would 'have a bloody day of it' defending the Queen against Essex's assault. Gorges claimed that Essex had 2,000 men with him; in fact there were 200. A musketeer, probably Sir Christopher Blount, fired four bullets at Raleigh; but the shots all missed. Armed men set out in another boat from Essex House, so Gorges pushed his cousin away. Raleigh rowed back to shore and escaped back to the Court. He had to protect the Queen and warn the Council.

Cecil sent some Privy Councillors to Essex to stop him from rebelling, but they were put in custody. Essex declared that there was a plot to kill him and hand over the country to Spain. Raleigh and Cecil were the ringleaders. The young earl mounted his horse and rode through the City of London, shouting: 'For the Queen! A plot is laid for my life!' The mob did not join him, and the Sheriff of London gave him no help. Cecil called him a traitor, and he fell back on Essex House, where he found that Gorges had released his hostages, the

A plan of the River Thames near Essex House, 1598.

Privy Councillors. Most of his leading supporters fled except for
Southampton and Blount. His enemy, the Lord Admiral Charles
Howard, Earl of Nottingham, led the soldiers that surrounded Essex
House and threatened to blow it up with gunpowder. Essex and his
remaining supporters surrendered and were charged with treason.

At his trial, Blount confessed that the Spanish plot of Raleigh and
Cecil was a fabrication. 'It was a word cast out to colour other matters.'
On the scaffold, Blount begged Raleigh's forgiveness, and Raleigh
willingly granted it to him and wished him the forgiveness of God.
Essex was insolent at his trial and sneered at Raleigh taking the oath
on the Bible as a witness. It was no use 'to swear the fox'. He was
finally sentenced to be beheaded, although Southampton was
reprieved.

As Captain of the Guard, Raleigh was present at his rival's execution
in the Tower of London. Before he died, Essex took back his
allegations against Raleigh and Cecil in a written confession. But he
could not ask for Raleigh's forgiveness on the scaffold. Some of his
friends were in the small crowd watching the execution, and they
voiced their anger that his enemy should be present. So Raleigh
walked away to the Armoury to watch the end of Essex from a
window. He did not hear Essex's request for a final reconciliation
with him.

Slander said that Raleigh lit a pipe and joked as the executioner
raised his axe and cut off Essex's head. This was not true. Raleigh's
withdrawal was proof of his discretion and powers of bleak reflection
that made him write his poem 'On the Life of Man':

> What is our life? A play of passion . . .
> Our graves that hide us from the searching Sun
> Are like drawn curtains when the play is done,
> Thus march we playing to our latest rest,
> Only we die in earnest, that's no Jest.

After all, Raleigh himself had been confined in the Tower. Essex's
fate might one day be his own.

IX

THE LAST YEARS OF GLORIANA

Essex had brought his death upon himself, yet Raleigh was held responsible for it. His brilliant, aloof character attracted evil reports. He was said to be the instigator of things which he had not done. He was held to be a schemer when he did not bother to scheme. He was too haughty to answer his enemies, too trusting to protect his position. His pride was, indeed, proverbial. He seemed to weather the years and the disasters that ruined others such as Essex. As one attack on him ran:

> Raleigh doth time bestride:
> He sits 'twixt wind and tide.
> Yet uphill he cannot ride
> For all his bloody pride.

The true schemer near the Queen, however, was Sir Robert Cecil. He was already preparing for the future when the Queen should die, as die she must. The Scottish ambassadors sent by King James VI to deal with Essex, whom James called 'my martyr', dealt secretly with Cecil. He assured them that he would work for King James's succession to the throne of England. He would keep constantly in touch with the Scottish Court. Nothing must be known, all must be hidden, because Queen Elizabeth hated anyone except herself dealing with the intolerable fact that someone else must wear the Crown after her.

Essex had finally cleared both Cecil and Raleigh of plotting with Spain. Now plotting with the Scottish King, Cecil made sure that Queen Elizabeth's likely successor would not believe in any such treason from her Principal Secretary. He did not, however, clear the name of Raleigh, who was too loyal to the Queen, too honest and too proud to insure himself against the future. Only once did he meet one of the Scottish nobles sent by King James to win powerful

Englishmen to his cause. But Raleigh refused to negotiate or to commit himself. He was the Queen's Captain of the Guard unto death.

In the last years of her reign, the Queen did restore Raleigh to favour. She knew that she could wholly depend on his service and allegiance. He felt secure, not only because of Her Majesty, but also because of his friendship with her Principal Secretary. Cecil's wife had died and his motherless young son Will stayed with Raleigh and his beloved wife at Sherborne for months on end. Raleigh was a second father to the boy. He counted on Cecil to support him without ever seeing in Cecil the shrewdness and duplicity of a man who wanted to govern England through any monarch, present Queen or future King. Power was more important to Cecil than affection. He would not put his friend before his will to rule his country.

Raleigh may have misunderstood the strength of his relationship with Cecil; but he completely misjudged the character of his new friend, Cecil's brother-in-law Henry Brooke, Lord Cobham, a vain, talkative, wealthy and cowardly man. Raleigh had secured for him the post of Warden of the Cinque Ports, an act which had confirmed Essex's suspicion that Raleigh and his friends were ready to deliver the coasts of England to a Spanish armada. Cobham was influential and was considered Raleigh's familiar – in one enemy's words, they were an 'accursed duality'. Cecil presented himself to King James as the one man able to keep Raleigh and Cobham from opposing the Scottish claim to the English throne. If he did not insist on King James's right of succession to these two 'gaping crabs, they would not stick to confess daily how contrary it is to their nature to be under your sovereignty'.

So Cecil secured his future with King James by damning his friend. Raleigh himself remained loyal to the Queen and her wishes, even in Parliament. He supported the Queen's demand for a subsidy needed to equip troops to fight off a Spanish landing in Ireland. He pointed out that the Queen was selling her jewels and rich clothes to raise money. Every patriotic Englishman should sacrifice something to help defend his country. Raleigh did not, however, approve of Cecil's comment that people should sell their pots and pans to raise pennies for the subsidy. In the Spaniards' eyes, such extreme acts would argue poverty in the state.

Raleigh was capable of a sacrificial gesture himself. When Parliament attacked the granting of monopolies to the Queen's favourites,

he offered to give up his patent on tin mining if all other patents were given up. The other possessors of monopolies were not so generous, and nothing was done to correct the abuse. Yet he had showed willing. And he spoke up, as always, for freedom of conscience and freedom from state intervention. He opposed a bill to force even Catholics to attend a Church of England service every Sunday. He also opposed bills to compel farmers to grow hemp for ship's rigging and to plough at least a third of their land for crops. Every farmer had the right to use his land as he thought best. The desire of a true Englishman was to be left free.

Raleigh's old interest in North America revived. He sent a small bark, the *Concord*, from Falmouth in 1602, carrying twenty-four gentlemen and eight sailors. They reached Cape Cod and Nantucket and set up a base on Cuttyhunk Island. They traded with the Indians and took aboard a cargo of furs, cedarwood and sassafras. Twelve of the gentlemen intended to remain as the nucleus of a colony, but they decided that their numbers were too few, their supplies insufficient. They sailed for home, but their report to Raleigh was the first English description of New England.

They found the coasts teeming with fish and game. Timber and vines and berries grew in profusion. The beaches were littered with the bones of whales. More interesting was the copper of the Indians and numerous glittering mineral stones. The earth was 'fat and lusty' and good for agriculture. The abundance of New England made the most fertile parts of old England appear barren. 'We stood awhile like men ravished at the beauty and delicacy of this sweet soil.' The local Indians were courteous, gentle and well-conditioned, excelling all the people of America.

So the first English report on New England reached Raleigh. It would attract later settlers there, the Pilgrims on the *Mayflower* who would follow to Massachusetts. As so often, Raleigh pointed the way without making a settlement or establishing a permanent presence. In fact, he withdrew from his venture in Ireland, selling off most of his estates. He could not defend or manage them. Ireland proved too much for him.

His lifelong hatred of Spain and love of seizing her wealth led him to send off more raiding ships from the West Country ports. Even Cecil joined in these ventures, although he did not want it known. Officially, he stood for better relations with Spain, as did King James, while Raleigh was known as Spain's inveterate enemy in his

Indians fishing. From Theodore de Bry, Americae Pars VIII . . ., *1599.*
By permission of the British Library.

'greediness for war'. Raleigh's religious tolerance did not extend to the fanatic Catholicism of Madrid. Brought up on Foxe's *Book of Martyrs* and tales of Protestants persecuted by the Spanish Inquisition, a witness to the cruelties practised in the name of rival Christian faiths in the wars in France and Ireland, he could never forget nor forgive the excesses of militant Catholic belief. Even when wisdom dictated that he should trim his sails to catch a fair wind from Spain, he could not change the hatred of a lifetime.

Nor could he change the love of a lifetime for enquiry and witty companions. Among Raleigh's intimate acquaintances and friends, John Aubrey numbered Ben Jonson, the playwright and leader of the group of writers who met at the Mermaid Tavern. Raleigh visited the Mermaid and would have met there Beaumont and Fletcher, Selden and John Donne. William Shakespeare, though, was Essex's

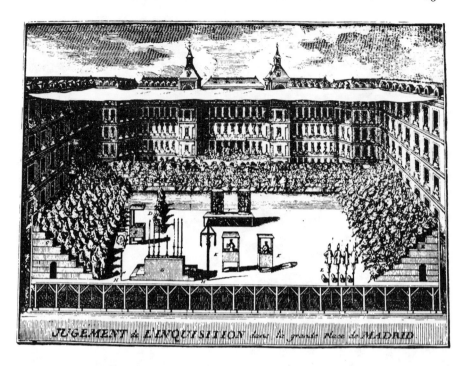

An eighteenth-century engraving of an auto-da-fé, *the public execution of Protestants and heretics condemned by the Inquisition in the main plaza in Madrid.*

and Southampton's man: his playing of *Richard the Second* on the eve of the rebellion had done him harm: he would not have joined Raleigh's company.

In her last months, Queen Elizabeth was heavy with silence and melancholy. She had no illness. She seemed to pine. She was no longer radiant, a Gloriana, but an old woman, plagued with troubles, at the end of a long reign. She wept at the anniversary of Essex's death. Her coronation ring grew too small for her swollen finger, and she had it filed off. She lay in her Bedchamber, waiting to die. Cecil asked her who should succeed, and she replied with little ambiguity, 'No base person, but a King.' It was a clear enough signal for James of Scotland.

The Queen died in March 1603. Raleigh clothed in black the Guard protecting the Queen's body until her funeral. There was no apparent

An engraving of Queen Elizabeth made in the last decade of her reign.
She is shown as the empress of the oceans.

opposition to the accession of King James of Scotland. Cecil had done much to arrange that. The new King rode slowly from Edinburgh towards London to take over his southern realm. Many noblemen rode out to meet him and swear their allegiance, but not Raleigh. He mourned the dead Queen who had lived through the rise of English sea power and maritime trade, the spread of discovery, the encounter of the peoples of Europe with those of the Americas, Asia and Africa. She had been the Cynthia, the Virginia, who had inspired Raleigh in his venturing, yet had summoned him back so often to her side. As he remembered in a poem:

> To seek new worlds, for gold, for praise, for glory,
> To try desire, to try love severed far,
> When I was gone she sent her memory
> More strong than were ten thousand ships of war,
> To call me back, to leave great honours thought,
> To leave my friends, my fortune, my attempt,
> To leave the purpose I so long had sought
> And hold both cares and comforts in contempt.

X

TIME OF TRIAL

Wʜᴇɴ ᴋɪɴɢ ᴊᴀᴍᴇѕ ʜᴀᴅ ʀᴇᴀᴄʜᴇᴅ Cecil's country mansion of Theobalds near London, Raleigh rode out to meet him. He was the stuff that legends are made of, and so his encounter with the new King became as legendary as his first encounter with the old Queen. The sight and the reputation of the tall and splendid knight from Devon seemed to offend the small, weak and paunchy King, whose tongue was too large for his mouth. 'On my soul, mon,' the King was said to say, 'I have heard *rawly* of thee.'

He had heard rawly of Raleigh. There were the accusations of Essex and his friends about the Spanish plot. There were Cecil's suggestions that Raleigh was, at best, a lukewarm supporter of the Scottish claim to the throne. And there were many English noblemen such as the Earl of Northumberland who used the change of the Crown to revenge themselves on somebody they had always considered an upstart, unduly favoured by Queen Elizabeth. Northumberland informed King James that Raleigh was insolent, extremely heated and not even influential. Whatever his appearance, he was not actually able to do the King much good or harm. Lord Henry Howard, though, considered Raleigh all powerful, a wizard and a magician who had cast spells to keep King James from the throne, 'the greatest Lucifer that hath lived in our age'.

So the King was prepared to think Raleigh insignificant and a demon. According to John Aubrey, the numbers of the English peers and gentry with Raleigh at Theobalds frightened King James. Secretly he dreaded their power and was inwardly envious. He told Raleigh that, if the English nobility had resisted his right to the throne, he would not have had the strength to insist on it.

'Would to God,' Raleigh replied, 'that had been put to the trial.'

'Why do you wish that?' the King asked.

Sir Walter Raleigh, 1588. By permission of the National Portrait Gallery.

'Because,' Raleigh said, 'that then you would have known your friends from your foes.'

If Raleigh did answer King James in such a bold and edged way, he could expect the King never to forget nor to forgive him. He was such a person, as Aubrey declared, that a Prince would rather be afraid of than ashamed of. 'He had that awfulness and ascendency in his Aspect over other mortals.' And King James did not intend to cringe.

For the time being the King professed to believe in Raleigh's allegiance. Raleigh was confirmed in his authority in the West Country, although he lost his chief source of income, his wine monopoly; for the King recalled all of Queen Elizabeth's grants of monopolies to her favourites. He would have the power of patronage. Raleigh also lost his position near the monarch's person: a Scot was made Captain of the Guard. Raleigh's reaction was characteristic, if not wise. He gave the King a pamphlet advocating a war with Spain in defence of the rebellious Protestant Netherlands. The King, however, wanted peace. He would not risk another armada against England.

The stripping of Raleigh's privileges and perquisites continued. The Bishop of Durham seized the opportunity to demand back his London house, which Queen Elizabeth had granted to Raleigh. The King ruled for the Bishop, and Raleigh was forced to evacuate all his possessions to Sherborne. It was a method of removing him from the centre of power in the capital. There were rumours of plots against the new King. There was also an accounting to be made against some of the leading and envied figures of the old régime.

Invited to join the Court for a hunting expedition at Windsor Castle, Raleigh was told by Cecil that the Privy Council wanted to question him. He was interrogated about contacts between his friend, Lord Cobham, and Count Aremberg, who represented the Spanish Netherlands. Did Raleigh know of a plot to remove the King and install the Roman Catholic faith in England? Raleigh denied any knowledge, but was sent to the Tower on a charge of treason. The indiscretion of his friends and the innuendoes of his enemies had persuaded the new Stuart King to destroy the chief ornament and support of the Tudor Crown.

Now it was Raleigh who was put to the trial. At last he would have to know his friends from his foes. Cecil had decided to sacrifice him. For his own reasons, he thought it necessary that Raleigh should fall as Essex had fallen, as an example to those who did not fully pledge themselves to the new King. He knew of two connected conspiracies, named the Bye and the Main Plots. The first was a plan by some priests and gentry to capture the King and force him to tolerate the Catholic faith: Lord Cobham's brother was involved in this. The Main Plot implicated Cobham himself, who disliked both Cecil and the new King. He had held frequent conferences with Count Aremberg and apparently proposed to finance a coup, by which King James's

cousin Arabella Stuart would be put on the throne, would accept Catholicism, and would marry a prince chosen by Spain – the very policy of Queen Mary Tudor.

Raleigh was involved because of his known friendship with Cobham. He was also denounced by Cobham's brother and later by Cobham himself, who kept on blaming Raleigh as the instigator of the plot, then retracting his allegations. An old charge against Raleigh, that of taking Spanish gold through Sarmiento de Gamboa, was revived: perhaps his expedition to Guiana had been in the interest of another country. Now Raleigh was accused of conspiring with the princely powers of Spain to bring about peace – King James's own policy. It was paradoxical, and, as Raleigh complained to Cecil, 'a heavy burden of God, to be in danger of perishing for a Prince which I have so long hated!'

Raleigh had little hope of a fair trial. While the Crown lawyers and prosecutors would misuse the law to bully the jury, the accused had to defend himself against charges that did not always require proof, since they were matters of state. Unless he could prove himself innocent, his guilt would be assumed. A charge of treason was enough to damn a man. It was certain that the King and his Council would want a conviction.

In the knowledge of his small chances of survival and of his fallen fortunes, Raleigh indulged in the dramatic gesture that was always part of the theatre of his life. He became strange and depressed. Then he plunged a knife into the right side of his chest, where his heart was not. He fell bleeding to the floor of his cell. When his gaolers rushed in, he protested his innocence. They bandaged him and hushed up the incident.

In agony of mind and body, Raleigh wrote to his wife. His words were wild with stress and sense of injury. He begged his wife to look after their son Wat and be charitable to the daughter born to him by Alice Goold. He denounced those who had testified falsely against him, particularly Lord Henry Howard. 'I am now made an enemy and traitor by the word of an unworthy man.' He prayed for the facts to be known. 'Oh God, thou dost know my wrongs, know then, thou my wife and child, know then, thou my Lord and King, that I ever thought them too honest to betray, and too good to conspire against.' His despair made him seek oblivion. 'Oh Death destroy my memory which is my Tormentor: my thoughts and my life cannot dwell in one body.'

It was poetic drama, the suicide attempt and the letter, the acting of a death to establish the truth when faced with actual death because of untruths. 'Only one dies in earnest,' Raleigh had written, 'that's no Jest.' Soon he recovered his usual courage and decided to resist. He refused to confess to any of his presumed crimes. He tried to give some of his courage to the wavering Lord Cobham, who was also imprisoned in the Tower. He advised his cowardly friend not even to confide in a preacher. Essex had done so and had made himself guilty. Cobham replied secretly, sending Raleigh a letter, which Raleigh kept as evidence that the charges against him were false.

His false friend Cecil pressed for Raleigh's conviction. His apostasy would prove to King James that Cecil would reject anybody for what he claimed as the good of the country – and the opportunity to remain the royal adviser. The French ambassador thought that Cecil was acting against Raleigh for his own interest and passion, not for the good of the kingdom. But the truth was more complex. Cecil was a man who believed in his own integrity and in reasons of state. And so he left Raleigh's fate to the law, which was the birthright of all Englishmen. He refused to intervene. If the laws against treason made a victim of the accused, that was no matter for Cecil.

A mob was incited to attack Raleigh on his way to his trial at Winchester. He was pelted with stones and abuse. Only his guards saved him. The Judges and commissioners appointed to try him were even more hostile. They included Cecil and Lord Henry Howard, while the prosecuting Attorney-General was the learned bully, Sir Edward Coke, whose ambition was greater than his service to justice. He would have the innocent convicted to secure his place in his profession.

Blustering and insinuating, Coke tried to declare Raleigh a traitor without proving it. He claimed that Raleigh was a member of the Bye Plot, when Raleigh had nothing to do with it. He claimed that the devilish and scheming Raleigh had sent Lord Cobham to intrigue with Count Aremberg in his place. He would prove his claims. 'Thou art a monster,' Coke said in Raleigh's face. 'Thou hast an English face, but a Spanish heart.'

Raleigh refused to lose his composure. He seemed detached, even amused. 'You fall out with yourself,' he told the raging Coke. 'I have said nothing to you. I am in no case to be angry.' When Coke shouted at him that he was a viper, the rankest traitor in all England, Raleigh replied quietly, 'No, no, Mr Attorney, I am no traitor. Whether I live

or die, I shall stand as true a subject as any the King hath. You may call me traitor at your pleasure; yet it becomes not a man of quality and virtue to do so. But I take comfort in it. It is all that you can do, for I do not yet hear that you charge me with any treason.'

Raleigh pointed out that he had defended England against Spain seven times, three times in Ireland, three at sea, once at Cadiz. He had spent his personal fortune equipping ships for the Royal Navy. How could he support a Spanish plot when he had recently given the King a pamphlet urging war on Spain? He was not so deluded as to think that the people would follow him in a rebellion. Essex had thought that. 'I was not such a madman,' Raleigh testified, 'as to make myself in this time a Robin Hood, a Wat Tyler, or a Jack Cade.'

Raleigh's chief accuser was Lord Cobham; but he had Cobham's letter sent to him in the Tower; it stated that Raleigh was as innocent and as clear from any treason against the King as any subject living. The possession of this letter gave Raleigh confidence. He insisted that Cobham should be called to the Court to testify against him in his presence. Coke and the Judges refused to allow this. They knew that Cobham might change his evidence, if he were to meet Raleigh face to face. He was not summoned to Winchester. Raleigh was to be condemned without a chance to question the leading witness against him. All the hearsay and evidence was distorted by Coke. Everything for him, Raleigh observed, was called cunning by Coke, while everything against him was called probable.

Both the prosecutor and the accused asked for the right to make the final speech to the jury.

'If you have done,' Raleigh said to Coke, 'then I have somewhat more to say.'

'Nay,' Coke replied, 'I will have the last word for the King.'

'Nay,' Raleigh said, 'I will have the last word for my life.'

The last word was not the last. Coke produced another letter written by Cobham to the House of Lords. It was dated after the letter sent to Raleigh in the Tower, excusing him from any taint of treason. Cobham now declared that Raleigh had asked him to approach Count Arem- berg for a pension of £1,500 a year for providing intelligence to Spain. The loss of his monopolies and privileges had left Raleigh short of funds. He had solicited, as he was accused of soliciting twenty years before, Spanish gold in order to act as a double agent.

Raleigh acknowledged that the pension had been offered to him through Cobham. He said he had declined it. He agreed that he

should have spoken of the offer and have admitted that Cobham had seen the Count who represented Spain. At the best, Raleigh was guilty of trying to conceal evidence that would certainly have been used against him. At the worst, he may have considered taking a Spanish pension – something that Sir Robert Cecil himself would take for the last eight years of his life. It was the Indian gold that Raleigh knew purchased intelligence, crept into Councils, and set bound loyalty free in the greatest monarchies.

There was still no evidence that Raleigh was guilty of treason. The case against him consisted of personal enmity, allegations, and the forsworn evidence of a contradictory friend Cobham, who had been threatened with torture. In his summing-up, the Lord Chief Justice made it plain that Raleigh was being condemned for what he was thought to be, not for what he was said to have done. He was denounced for being irreligious and wicked and proud, for his presumed faults of character rather than for being an actual traitor.

Nothing became Raleigh so much as his conduct at his trial. If he went into the Court innocent, but hated for his arrogance, he emerged condemned, but loved for his behaviour and pitied for the injustice of the verdict. Danger had brought out the best qualities in him. His sense of himself as the hero in the drama of his life made him act as the hero when that life was under threat. 'Sir Walter Raleigh served for a whole act,' Sir Dudley Carleton wrote, 'and played all the parts himself.' He seemed to glory in his performance. He answered his accusers 'with that temper, wit, learning, courage, and judgement, that, save it went with the hazard of his life, it was the happiest day that ever he spent'.

So Raleigh acted in the best spirit of the Elizabethan era and of the Age of Discovery. He showed his great qualities at his worst time of trial, showing such grace under pressure that he changed the opinion of his countrymen. His gallant defence of himself against the unjust charges of the Crown had made him seem a martyr for the liberties and the laws of England. He was the victim of royal persecution. His long service in Parliament made him appear a sacrifice to free speech and honest patriotism. If he had been thought too proud before, he was too popular now. It might be that King James would not dare to have him executed for the traitor he evidently was not.

XI

THE TOWER YEARS

Raleigh's composure at his trial did not endure. The conspirators of the Bye Plot were horribly executed. Raleigh's wife Bess implored Cecil to save her husband, while Raleigh himself wrote letters to King James and to the Lords, begging for his life. But as the day of his execution approached, his courage returned. He wrote to his wife, asking her to retrieve his letters pleading for mercy. He would die boldly. 'Know it, dear wife, that your son is the child of a true man, and who, in his own respect, despiseth Death and all his misshapen and ugly forms.'

An Elizabethan father instructing his wife and children in religious matters.
From The Whole Psalms in Four Parts, *1563.*

Raleigh showed himself to be a Christian as he faced his end. The Bishop who attended him believed he was. 'Bless my poor boy,' Raleigh implored his wife. 'Pray for me. My true God hold you both in His arms.' He wrote his most religious poem, 'The Passionate Man's Pilgrimage'. It describes his long journey through life as a journey towards more blessed paths. In heaven, there will be:

> No Conscience molten into gold,
> No forged accusers bought and sold . . .

Even the final stroke of the axe on his neck will be the setting of an everlasting head on his soul. After his turbulent life, there will be peace for the passionate pilgrim.

> Give me my Scallop shell of quiet,
> My staff of Faith to walk upon,
> My Scrip of Joy, Immortal diet,
> My bottle of salvation:
> My Gown of Glory, hope's true gage,
> And thus I'll take my pilgrimage.

He had many years to wait before he could set out on his pilgrimage. King James showed mercy, refined by cruelty. Raleigh was told to wait at his prison window which overlooked the scaffold. Lord Cobham and two other condemned conspirators were led one by one to the block. They were allowed to make their last prayers. On the point of execution, they were told that they were reprieved for two hours. Finally, they were summoned to the scaffold together, denounced for their crimes and informed that the King had granted them their lives. They were to be exiled or imprisoned.

This black comedy of compassion, this jest of death made, as Carleton wrote, hammers work in Raleigh's head to beat out the meaning of this stratagem. Would the King play with him as with the others, cat and mouse? The King did, commuting Raleigh's sentence to imprisonment in the Tower.

Stone walls did a prison make for Raleigh, but iron bars did not cage his spirit. He used his captivity to pursue his experiments in botany, medicine and science. His ambition also led him to begin writing a mammoth *History of the World*. His powers of persuasion gave him privileges in the Tower, where his wife and child were allowed to stay with him. He even managed to preserve some of his estates for them through the ambiguous grace of Cecil.

Astrologers and astronomers in Raleigh's time.
From Robert Fludd, Utriusque Cosmi Historia, *1617.*

Although more than fifty years of age, crippled and often ill from the dampness of the Tower, Raleigh was no spent force. He was a living symbol of past greatness and present royal injustice. His cheerful and humble and hard-working life made people forget his pride and remember his services to his country. He was to be seen conducting botanical experiments in a small garden granted to him by the Lieutenant of the Tower. He planted seeds and watched their growth. He used herbs and minerals to make remedies. One of these,

his 'elixir of life' or royal cordial, became a famous cure for fevers. It remained in common use for over a century.

Raleigh also changed a hen-house against the Tower wall into a laboratory. There he spent many of his days refining and assaying ores, including samples he had brought over from Guiana. He also distilled chemicals and potions. He was known as a great chemist and thought to be an alchemist. The legend that he was a magician still lingered. His reputation grew with his enforced seclusion.

An alchemist in his laboratory in the eyes of popular opinion.
From Heinrich Khunrath, Amphitheatrum Aeternae Sapientiae, *1609.*

When the Gunpowder Plot to blow up the Houses of Parliament was discovered in 1605, Raleigh was still thought powerful and dangerous enough to be involved. He was questioned by the House of Lords, but his innocence was beyond doubt. His popularity grew in admiration of his endurance. The Danish Queen Anne was cured by Raleigh's royal cordial and interceded for him with her husband, King James, who would not listen. Her brother, the King of Denmark, wanted Raleigh released to become an admiral in his navy, but King James would not risk freeing his famous prisoner. He feared him too much.

He also hated Raleigh for the practice that he had introduced, the art of smoking. Raleigh's chief consolation was his pipe of tobacco.

A contemporary engraving of Sir Walter Raleigh.

Smoking in the theatre during the reign of King James.
From the title page of The Roaring Girl, *1611.*

He had set a fashion for smoking in Court and country, even though good tobacco was worth, weight for weight, as much as gold. The King might hardly ever wash or change his clothes. He might drink too much whisky, but he abhorred tobacco and the man who had brought it to England. Smoking was a vile and stinking custom, the King wrote, 'loathsome to the eye, hateful to the nose, harmful to the brain, dangerous to the lungs'.

Raleigh still lit his pipe and remained in the Tower at the King's pleasure. Other men were following the paths of his pioneering and his pilgrimage. Colonies were again being attempted in North America, backed by Raleigh's relatives and Judges. Sir Humphrey Gilbert's sons, Sir Ferdinando Gorges and the Lord Chief Justice at Raleigh's trial helped to found the Plymouth Company, intended to

colonize New England. A group of London merchants also founded
a company to settle Virginia. Instructed by Hakluyt's works and the
reports of Raleigh's missions, the *Godspeed*, the *Susan Constant* and
the *Discovery* were sent out with colonists to found Jamestown in
Virginia.

Even though confined to the Tower, Raleigh was asked to advise
the settlers and the beginnings of the first township in the New
World. He had named the territory Virginia in honour of his dead
Queen, and Virginia it was always to be called. A friend, the poet
Michael Drayton, wrote an ode to the voyage of 1606. He honoured
Raleigh's pioneer spirit as much as those that sailed upon it:

> You brave heroic minds
> Worthy your country's name,
> That honour still pursue,
> Go and subdue . . .
>
> And cheerfully at sea,
> Success you still entice,
> To get the pearl and gold
> And ours to hold,
> Virginia,
> Earth's only Paradise.

So began 'the planting of nations' that was to originate the United
States of America, and that Raleigh thought so important in his
History of the World. The migration of peoples and their settlement in
other lands was the course of history. Raleigh's immense project
began with an account of the Creation and was intended to reach his
own days. He had the time for study enforced on him, and he had the
help of Ben Jonson and 'the best wits of England'. Yet it was a
mammoth undertaking, and in seven years he wrote a million words,
his global judgement from the Creation to the conquest of Macedon
by Rome.

He presented history as the unfolding of the divine purpose
through human actions. 'God, who is the author of all our tragedies,
hath written out for us and appointed us all the parts we are to play.'
Irremediable time is also the destroyer of empires and individuals.
'This tide of man's life, after it once turneth and declineth, ever
runneth with a perpetual ebb and falling stream, but never floweth
again: our leaf once fallen, springeth no more.' The wicked, however,
are punished more harshly than the innocent. Even tyrannical kings

meet their doom. A just God raises and throws down 'Kings, Estates, Cities, and Nations, for the same offences which were committed of old, and are committed in the present'. By implication, even King James would be judged.

Although Raleigh's *History of the World* was written about the centuries before Christ, he constantly used examples from his own experience. When he tried to describe the Garden of Eden, he also described the rich soil he had seen in Guiana. When speculating about the Tree of Knowledge, he mentioned the fig trees bearing oysters that he had noticed by the Orinoco River. He referred to the religious wars in France and his attack on Fayal. History and its making was something in which he had played his part.

Above all, the *History of the World* showed the values of loyalty and constancy and right dealing. Flattery was useless, even for courtiers. It was not enough 'to be wise with a wise Prince, valiant with a valiant, and just with him that is just'. For every Prince had to have a successor. And if that successor were different in character, then the courtier had to 'sail with the tide of the time, and alter form and condition'. Cecil had done so and still served King James. Raleigh had not done so and served in the Tower. Yet providence would judge them all, and finally death, 'eloquent, just and mighty Death, whom none could advise', but who had drawn together 'all the far-stretched greatness, all the pride, cruelty and ambition of man, and covered it all over with these two narrow words, *Hic Jacet*', Here He Lies!

Raleigh's *History of the World* was like his life, vast in scope and risk, protean and enquiring, full of strange learning and intriguing experience, wise and wayward, shrewd and reflective, original and provoking, fluent and sonorous, written with the pen of a recording angel about the greatness and follies of people and the necessities of man's fate that the author called providence. Raleigh had the spirit to try everything and discover anything. Excess was his continual attempt. His history of mankind still shows how far he reached and how much he encompassed. No other man has achieved so ranging a work from a prison cell.

XII

LAWLESS LIBERTY

Raleigh had received the Sherborne estate from the favour of Queen Elizabeth. He was to lose Sherborne to the new favourite of King James. Robert Carr, a young and handsome Scotsman, broke a leg in the tilting yard and lay before the King's admiring eyes. Soon he was always at the King's side. He was created a knight and eventually the Earl of Somerset. He did not possess a country estate, and Cecil suggested that the King grant him Sherborne. There was a flaw in the title deed, by which Raleigh had conveyed the estate to his son Wat before the treason trial. Thus the estate was technically forfeit to the Crown, which had the right to seize all the possessions of a condemned traitor.

The King and Cecil did not dare to proceed with the outright confiscation of Sherborne. Lady Raleigh was forced to accept £8,000 for the estate with an annual pension of £400 for life. It was a petty price, not enough. She threw herself upon her knees in front of the King, beseeching him not to expose herself and her children to ruin and beggary. But the King passed her by, muttering, 'I mun have the land, I mun have it for Carr.'

Raleigh himself wrote to Carr from the Tower, asking him not to take over Sherborne. He had suffered every loss. This one would be the last fatal blow. 'Seeing your day is but now in the dawn and mine coming to the evening,' Raleigh wrote to the new royal favourite, 'I beseech you not to begin your first building upon the ruins of the innocent.' He warned Carr to avoid the curse on those who took the inheritance of the defenceless. Instead, Carr took Sherborne.

Raleigh now had to provide for two sons. His baby Carew had been conceived in the Tower during one of his wife's visits. Raleigh had nothing more to leave to his children. Yet he had one hope, the support of Prince Henry, the heir to the throne. As with so many sons of monarchs, Prince Henry seemed to prize the counsel and company

of the man most feared by his father. A Prince may not oppose a King, but he may make friends with the King's opponents in order to assert his difference.

Raleigh began writing policy papers for the King's son. The first ones advised against any marriage to a Catholic or Spanish princess. The others dealt with trade and commerce, the rise of great cities, the workings of government, military and naval matters, the soul and scepticism, and the Norman kings. It was a course of instruction with a purpose. Raleigh intended to become the counsellor of the next King of England, who might restore him to his former glories. Prince Henry even attacked his father on the grant of Sherborne to Carr and demanded the estate for himself. His father bought off Carr and gave the estate to his son. Raleigh believed his royal pupil would bestow it on him, once he was released from the Tower.

Raleigh's position was peculiar. He was a condemned traitor, yet a trusted adviser to the heir to the throne. The Privy Council itself became concerned with his influence and decided to examine him again. It was discovered that his many years in prison had not broken his spirit. 'We find no change,' his enemy Lord Henry Howard had to admit, 'but the same boldness, pride, and passion.' He would be reported for these faults to the King. Eight years in gaol had not tamed his free spirit in 'the lawless liberty of the Tower'.

Cecil might have been expected to outlive his old imprisoned friend, but he died in 1612 at the age of forty-eight. He suffered from many of the diseases of the time and appeared worn out. His death was followed that same year by another death that killed off Raleigh's hopes. Prince Henry swam in the filthy Thames, caught typhoid fever, recovered and relapsed. The agonized Queen sent for Raleigh's royal cordial. The Prince drank it, revived, then died. Raleigh's dark warning was heard, that the cordial would only cure the Prince if he had not already been poisoned.

Raleigh had dedicated his *History of the World* to Prince Henry, and now he lost interest in finishing it. It was to have been his ultimate instruction on the workings of providence to the future King. He wanted to play Aristotle to another Alexander the Great. The Prince had died, however, and Raleigh's chances of recovering Sherborne (now granted back to Carr) and of becoming a royal counsellor again were for ever gone.

The unfinished *History of the World* was published, then temporarily banned by order of the King. Although there were no direct attacks

The Tower of London where Raleigh was imprisoned for thirteen years.
From Visscher's Panorama of London, *1618.*

on him, he sensed that Raleigh did speak out too much against royal authority in time past. But the ban was lifted, and the *History* was printed in many editions, which influenced such men as John Milton and John Hampden, Oliver Cromwell and John Locke. King James was correct. Raleigh's words from the Tower were construed as an assault on the divinity and righteousness of kingship. For the *History* did emphasize the working out of God's plans and the punishment of the unjust. However high and mighty a man, there would be retribution for doing wrong. God ruled all and through all. His secret will was the cause of everything. 'God worketh by Angels, by the Sun, by the Stars, by Nature, and by men.'

Providence seemed to work at last in Raleigh's defence. Carr, now Earl of Somerset, and the Howard family became involved in one of the more notorious poisoning cases in English history. The executed Earl of Essex's son had been persuaded into a dynastic marriage at the age of fourteen with Lady Frances Howard, the daughter of

Raleigh's fellow commander, Lord Thomas Howard, and the niece of Raleigh's enemy, Lord Henry Howard. Because the Earl of Essex was so young, the marriage was not consummated. Lady Frances was ambitious and saw that Robert Carr was the chief source of royal patronage. She consulted witches and astrologers, who gave her potions to make her young husband impotent. She requested a divorce from him and was granted it by a commission of bishops appointed by King James.

While waiting for the divorce, Carr confided in a close friend, the writer Thomas Overbury, who despised Lady Frances and warned Carr against the marriage. The Howard family was so angry at Overbury that they persuaded the King to send him abroad and then commit him to the Tower. There he was poisoned by food sent to him by Lady Frances. Rumours spread, and the King was growing weary of his favourite and the scandals attached to his name. Sir Edward Coke was loosed on the case. The Lieutenant of the Tower confessed to the poison plot. Carr and Lady Frances were condemned to death, but she was pardoned before joining her husband in the Tower. Lord Henry Howard died, while the Howard family and the dead Cecil were proved to have been accepting pensions from Spain for many years – the accusation that had falsely made Raleigh seem a traitor.

The absolute downfall of his enemies appeared to prove Raleigh's belief in the workings of providence. The wicked were punished. Now it only remained for the innocent to be freed. The King took a new favourite, George Villiers, later created Duke of Buckingham, who seized the opportunity to urge hostilities against treacherous Spain, the corrupter of the King's Council. King James was also short of funds as he had seriously depleted the royal revenues and did not want to summon Parliament and beg them for subsidies. Raleigh took the chance and urged his old project of the empire of Guiana and the quest for El Dorado. It would both strike at Spain and fill the royal coffers. He would rather, he wrote, die for the King, and not by the King.

In 1616, after spending thirteen years in the Tower, Sir Walter Raleigh was released at the age of sixty-four, sickly, crippled in one leg, and partially paralysed from a stroke in his left side. Poetic justice made his old Tower rooms the new home of Carr and Lady Frances Howard. Raleigh had survived the persecution of his enemies to lead a last expedition in search of the grand illusion of a golden city that never was, yet might be.

XIII

THE KNIGHT OF EL DORADO

As the *History of the World* NOTED, many Spaniards had spent their labour, their wealth and their lives in search of a golden kingdom. And some had found it. 'They are worthily rewarded,' Raleigh wrote, 'with these Treasuries and Paradises which they enjoy.' These were rare kind words from Spain's notorious enemy, but they had their purpose. Raleigh had never given up his dream of founding an empire in Guiana and bringing back a shipload of gold. During his years in the Tower, he had begged Cecil to back an expedition to the Orinoco and had invested himself in Sir Thomas Roe's failed attempt to discover El Dorado in 1609; Roe had returned with more tales of gold mines and no precious metal. Yet Raleigh was sure the gold was there: his man Lawrence Keymis had seen a mine at the river mouth. He knew his need to satisfy King James that 'his design was not imaginary but true'.

Certainly, Raleigh believed in the truth of his expedition. He persuaded his wife to invest much of the £8,000 received for Sherborne and the proceeds of the sale of her Mitcham estate. He enlisted his elder son Wat as one of his commanders 'in hope of enriching them by the mines of Guiana'. Outside forty other gentlemen, his means only allowed him to recruit 'the very scum of the world' to man his ships. But he pressed on with his preparations, confident in one last miracle of energy and good fortune. He did not choose to see the peril that threatened him, although he knew the odds against his success. 'Being old and sickly, thirteen years in prison, and not used to the air, to travel, and to watching', it was ten to one that he would never return.

Perhaps the King did not mean him to return. It was surprising that he let Raleigh go at all. King James was playing both sides of the coin. He satisfied George Villiers and the anti-Spanish party by sending out the old venturer on his last quest. If, against all odds,

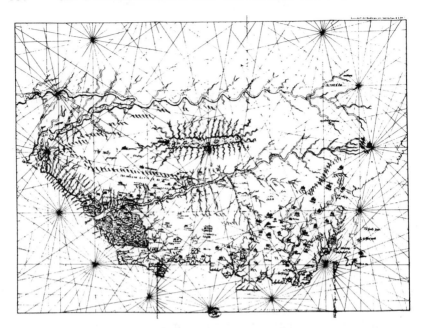

A contemporary German map based on Raleigh's first voyage to Guiana.
Manoa (El Dorado) is marked on a mountain lake shaped like a centipede between
the Orinoco and Amazon Rivers. By permission of the British Library.

Raleigh did bring back a treasure trove from Guiana, then he would solve the problems of the exchequer as Drake had done for Queen Elizabeth. If Raleigh failed, he would either die in the Caribbean, sparing the King the embarrassment of having him executed, or he would return to be accused twice of treason for having tried to start an unlawful war against Spain.

For the King had not pardoned Raleigh. He was let out of the Tower on trial. The conditions imposed on his mission to Guiana were intolerable. Another Sarmiento, Count Gondomar, was Spanish ambassador in London: he was a relative of the Pedro Sarmiento de Gamboa who had first incited Raleigh with stories of the riches of El Dorado. Gondomar was an intimate of the King and often presented him with rich gifts. He protested that Guiana belonged to Spain and not to the English Crown as Raleigh claimed. He asserted that Raleigh wanted to play the pirate, not to look for gold mines. So he persuaded

the King to give Raleigh a commission preventing him from taking any Spanish lives or property during his search in Guiana 'under peril of the law'.

Raleigh accepted the commission, believing Keymis's claim that there was no Spanish settlement near the gold mines. He also knew that if he did attack the silver fleet and return with a fortune, he would be forgiven. 'Did you ever hear of any,' he joked to the Lord Chancellor Francis Bacon, 'that was counted a pirate for taking millions?' But if he broke the straitjacket of his commission and did not return with a king's ransom, he was doomed, and he knew it.

He gave a further hostage to fortune. The King demanded a full account of all Raleigh's seven major vessels, his armament, his route and his sailing dates. This information was secretly given to Gondomar, who sent it to Madrid. It was then passed on to the Spanish Caribbean empire, where the authorities knew exactly Raleigh's strength and likely time of arrival. The Spaniards still remained unsure of his real intentions, fearing an attack on Genoa. But his flagship *Destiny* led out his little fleet bound for Guiana in June 1617. Contrary winds blew him back to Falmouth, then later to Ireland; but by September, he reached the Canary Islands, where he refused to retaliate after three of his men were ambushed and killed by the Spaniards. He knew that he was in peril of the law for any assault on Spain. Unfortunately, one of his captains, stopped by Raleigh from piracy, deserted and returned to London and accused Raleigh of piracy himself. It was a lie, but it was believed.

Disease, storms and calms plagued the fleet as it crossed the Atlantic. Raleigh himself was stricken by fever, while nearly 100 of his 1,000 men died. At last the expedition reached the mouth of the Orinoco, where the gold mines were to be found, where an English empire was to be established in the wilderness.

A Spanish settlement named San Tomé was already there. Raleigh referred to it scornfully as a town of sticks covered with the leaves of trees and defended by a wooden fort. Yet it was evidence of Spanish occupation and posed a threat to an English landing. Raleigh knew that the Spaniards could not 'endure that the English nation should look upon any part of America', which was more than a quarter of the known world. But they did not possess Guiana, being hated by the Indians, who had looked to Raleigh twenty-two years before as their protector against Spanish cruelty and had pledged their allegiance to the English Crown. In Raleigh's opinion, the Spaniards were inter-

lopers at San Tomé: their right to be there was mere force. King James had the best and most Christian title to the empire of Guiana, because 'the natural lords did most willingly acknowledge Queen Elizabeth to be their sovereign'.

So Raleigh justified his breach of the conditions of his mission. He could not be bound by them, because he was doomed as a bankrupt traitor if he returned without gold. 'There is no middle course,' he had written to a friend before sailing, 'but perish or prosper.' He ordered Lawrence Keymis, his nephew George Raleigh, and his headstrong son Wat to land with 4,000 men between San Tomé and the site of the presumed gold mine, to collect some ore for assaying, and to defend themselves if attacked by the garrison of the Spanish town. He himself was too weak from fever to leave the *Destiny*. He would remain in command of his fleet, expecting an attack from Spanish galleons forewarned of his arrival. He would fight to the death as the *Revenge* had. Rather than surrender, he would burn his ships to ashes. 'Run away I will never.'

While Keymis led the landing force, Raleigh cruised off Trinidad. He sent his men ashore to exploit the great lake of pitch, so useful for coating wooden ships. He also had them search for tropical plants and roots which he needed in order to concoct his special medicines and cordials. And he waited for news from the mouth of the Orinoco River, a confirmation of the gold mine that could not be a fantasy. If it were, his ruin was certain.

On 13 February 1618, Raleigh received a message of disaster. Keymis reported on what he and his men had done. They had landed near San Tomé and had been ambushed by the Spaniards, who had nearly routed them. Wat Raleigh had led a counterattack, which had driven the enemy back to the edge of the town. There, Francis Bacon later declared, Wat had cried out, 'Come on, my hearts, here is the mine that you must expect. They that look for any other mine are fools.' It was evidence that Wat did not believe in his father's dream of El Dorado. He had dashed ahead, seeking his violent destiny and his father's doom. He was shot in the body by a musket ball and had his skull broken by a musket butt. Dying, he had shouted, 'Go on! The Lord have mercy upon me, and prosper your enterprise.'

Keymis pressed the assault and took San Tomé. It was a bloody encounter. The English lost four of their officers and the Spaniards lost five. Keymis discovered no gold in the town although he did find three or four refiners' houses. The gold mines were said to be

NEVVES
Of Sr. Walter Rauleigh.

WITH
The true Defcription of GVIANA:

As alfo a Relation of the excellent Gouernment, and much hope of the profperity of the Voyage.

Sent from a Gentleman of his Fleet, to a moſt eſpeciall Friend of his in London.

From the Riuer of Caliana, *on the Coaſt of* Guiana, *Nouemb.* 17. 1617.

LONDON,
Printed for *H. G.* and are to be fold by *I. Wright,* at the figne of the Bible without New-gate. 1618.

A pamphlet written during Raleigh's second voyage to Guiana, 1617.

anything from 200 to 400 miles from San Tomé. Keymis left a garrison in the town and sailed up the Orinoco, fired at by Spaniards from the banks and islands in the river. He lost many men, found no mines and no gold, and came back downriver to discover that his garrison had panicked and had burned San Tomé to the ground. With less than half his men, Keymis returned to account to Raleigh, who was bitter with loss and grief.

Keymis tried to make his excuses. The Spaniards had attacked them first. The snipers from the banks of the Orinoco had prevented his men from forcing their way to the actual gold mine. The burning of San Tomé had contradicted his orders. But Raleigh would not listen to these reasons. His son was dead and could not be brought back. Keymis should have lost another hundred men and reached the gold mine at all costs. The destruction of the Spanish town was unforgivable. Keymis apologized, but Raleigh would not 'favour or colour in any sort his former folly'. Keymis said, 'I know then, Sir, what course to take.' He left Raleigh's cabin and went up to his own. There he shot himself in the ribs with a pistol and stabbed himself in the heart with a long knife.

Keymis's suicide confirmed his commander's ruin. Raleigh wrote back to his wife about their son's death and the second death that awaited him on his return to England. 'Comfort your heart, dear Bess. I shall sorrow for us both; and I shall sorrow the less because I have not long to sorrow, because not long to live . . . My brains are broken, and it is a torment for me to write.'

Raleigh was in such despair that he lost his authority. His captains would not obey him and mount another expedition to search for the gold mines. They were afraid that a Spanish fleet was at sea, sent to destroy them. Some deserted to look for prizes on the Spanish main, others insisted on sailing back to England. Raleigh talked of going to Newfoundland to victual his ships before ambushing the annual silver convoy from the Americas, but these were the last hopes of a man who had lost all in pursuit of the fantasy of El Dorado.

El Dorado was not entirely fantasy. There had been a gold-rich Indian tribe which had performed ceremonies and sunk precious objects in the mountain lakes of Siecha and Guatavita. There were gold-bearing rocks in Guiana. Raleigh had samples of them from his previous expedition: the precious metal has since been extracted from the stones of Mount Iconuri near San Tomé. Yet Raleigh could not prove that. As Francis Bacon's *Declaration* against him was to state,

Raleigh had so enchanted the world with his confident assertions of what every man was willing to believe, that King James himself had been misled in the hope of great riches and noble enterprises 'for plantations, discoveries, and opening of new trades'.

Raleigh, though, had misled himself more than any other man. Although old and sick, he still believed almost mystically in his power and his energy. His friends John Dee and Thomas Hariot asserted that a man of strong desire could use cosmic forces to achieve human ends. Raleigh knew that he possessed that strong desire, that he was the last heir to the heightened Elizabethan sense of adventure and defiance, courage and questing, through which a man could transcend his own limits and the limits of the known world. His was the poetry of empire, the theatre of rich discovery. To him, Guiana was the Garden of Eden as well as a tropical delta, while El Dorado was a fact as well as a golden dream. He acted his imagination, he played many parts in the drama he made of his life that culminated in a last fated role in search of a lost city never to be found.

The *Destiny* sailed back alone to Ireland, then on to Plymouth. Raleigh did not choose to avoid his fate. 'I returned to England,' he wrote, 'with manifest peril of my life, with a purpose not to hold my life with any other than his majesty's grace.' No one could persuade him to flee to France, even though the King might well hand him over to the Spanish authorities to be hanged in Madrid. His last act had failed. His life seemed wretched. He had risked all and endeavoured all and lost all.

Two centuries later, Edgar Allan Poe would write of him as the Knight of El Dorado. The poem illuminated that strange quest for real gold and dream gold, for present fame and immortality, that has made the name of Sir Walter Raleigh seem extraordinary to this day – Poe's gallant knight:

> But he grew old –
> This knight so bold –
> And o'er his heart a shadow
> Fell as he found
> No spot of ground
> That looked like Eldorado.
>
> And, as his strength
> Failed him at length,
> He met a pilgrim shadow –

'Shadow,' said he,
'Where can it be –
This land of Eldorado?'

'Over the Mountains
Of the Moon,
Down the Valley of the Shadow,
Ride, boldly ride,'
The shade replied, –
'If you seek for Eldorado!'

XIV

FACING DEATH

'Pirates! pirates! pirates!'
gondomar shouted at King James on hearing of the burning of
San Tomé. The King issued a proclamation inviting testimony against
Raleigh and accusing him of breaking the peace with Spain.
Gondomar pressed for Raleigh to be sent to Madrid for judgement,
but finally royal pride and the Privy Council refused to hand over
a national hero to foreign punishment. 'I may as well hang him as
deliver him to the King of Spain,' King James was persuaded to say,
'and one of these two I must do.'

Raleigh was not arrested on his arrival in Plymouth. His wife came
to meet him and warn him of reprisals threatened from London. She
wanted him to flee to France, but he would not. He still believed that
he could justify his doings in Guiana. A cousin, Sir Lewis Stukeley,
Vice-Admiral of Devon, was ordered to arrest him and bring him to
London. With him was a French doctor, Manourie, who aided Raleigh
to play a last comic interlude in the final act of his life.

Raleigh needed time to use his pen and write an *Apology* for what
he had done on the expedition. Only his wits and his nerve could
save him now. So, in Salisbury, he convinced Manourie to give him
an emetic and a poisonous ointment that reddened his skin and
blistered it with purple spots. He pretended to be violently ill and
insane. It gave him several days to write his *Apology*. He excused his
stratagem by saying that King David in the Bible had feigned
madness, but God had forgiven him.

The *Apology* probed at the weakness in the case against him. If
Guiana was a possession of the English Crown, then Raleigh had
been right in going there, in attacking Spanish interlopers, and in
searching for gold mines. If it was not English territory, then King
James should never have permitted the expedition in the first place.
'If Guiana be not His Majesty's,' Raleigh wrote, 'the working of a

mine there and the taking of a town there had been equally perilous. For by doing the one I had robbed the King of Spain and been a thief, and by the other a disturber or breaker of the peace.' It was not possible, however, to break the peace with Spain in the Caribbean, because no peace was possible. The English had either to defend their rights to trade and colonize, or 'for ever abandon the Indies, and lose all our knowledge and our pilotage of that part of the world'.

King James seemed ready to do that. He had promised the Spaniards to give them Raleigh's head, and he would keep his promise because of Raleigh's manifest failure. Only he meant to give Raleigh the opportunity to put his own head in the noose. On arrival in London, Raleigh was not committed to the Tower, but allowed to stay in lodgings in the City. Discouraged by lack of any support from the Privy Council, he decided to flee to France in an English ketch. He confided his plan to his cousin Stukeley, still his official keeper. He believed blood was thicker than royal favour.

Stukeley betrayed him. Wearing a false beard and a large hat, Raleigh was rowed down the Thames in a small boat towards the ketch at Tilbury. They were followed by a larger boat which they could not escape. Near Greenwich, the pursuing boat came up and forced them to land. Then Stukeley arrested Raleigh in the name of the King. Cousin had deceived cousin. 'Sir Lewis,' Raleigh said, 'these actions will not turn out to your credit.' Stukeley received £1,000 from the King for his services and the name of Sir Judas.

Raleigh was rowed back under a small escort to be imprisoned again in the Tower. He was doomed. His bungled flight to France made him seem a double traitor. The King even tried to show contempt for his old adversary, claiming that Raleigh was a coward to be taken so easily. He might have escaped from the two men who guarded him on his way to the Tower. Such an escape would have relieved the King from the embarrassment of having Raleigh executed; but it was not attempted. Raleigh had decided to meet his destiny well.

The King still found it difficult to have Raleigh's head. He could ignore the appeals of his rejected Queen Anne, to whom Raleigh wrote a poem:

> If I have sold my duty, sold my faith
> To strangers, which was only due to one,
> No thing I should esteem so dear as Death.

He had not sold his faith to strangers. He was falsely accused. Only the Queen's intercession could save him.

> O had Truth Power the guiltless could not fall,
> Malice win Glory, or Revenge triumph;
> But Truth alone can not encounter all.
>
> Mercy is fled to God which Mercy made,
> Compassion dead, Faith turned to Policy,
> Friends know not those who sit in Sorrow's shade.
>
> For what we sometime were we are no more,
> Fortune hath changed our shape, and Destiny
> Defaced the very form we had before.

The Queen could not save Raleigh. He was accused of piracy against Spain, of trespassing on its territory, and of plotting with the French. Six Commissioners, including Sir Edward Coke and Francis Bacon, were appointed to examine the evidence. Raleigh had committed no actual acts of piracy. He had stopped his captains from turning pirate, and although he had talked of seizing the Spanish treasure fleet, he had not proceeded. If Guiana was English territory, as Raleigh asserted, then he had not trespassed against Spain. The Commissioners tried to prove that the gold mine near San Tomé had always been a fiction and a lure, but Raleigh had taken out mining equipment and had believed in its existence. As for conspiring with the French, Raleigh had returned to England before his last attempt at flight. He had not sailed the *Destiny* to a French port, but to Plymouth. He had trusted in the King's mercy, which was being denied to him.

The Commissioners made no progress in fabricating a case against Raleigh. They set an informer on to him, the Lieutenant of the Tower, to report on the prisoner, who was discreet and immersed in his scientific enquiries. The informer achieved nothing except exasperation at his captive's concentration on his experiments. Raleigh seemed devoted to his chemical stuffs, among which there were 'so many spirits of things' that only one appeared to be missing, the Spirit of God.

Without new evidence, the Commissioners were compelled to recommend to King James that Raleigh should be executed under the judgement from his previous treason trial. He had never been pardoned, even though released to go to Guiana. Otherwise, another public treason trial would be necessary. The King, however, did not

dare risk the second course. He remembered how Raleigh had changed opinion by his brilliant defence of himself at his trial fifteen years before, turning the hatred of men into compassion. So the King ordered Raleigh to be called in front of the Commissioners at a closed hearing. He defended himself with dignity, but there was no defence to be made. The issue was prejudged. He was sentenced to be beheaded.

He had, however, to appear in open court to receive his sentence. He was an old and ill man, white-haired and shaking with fever, lame and bent. He was hardly recognizable as the gallant knight in silver armour, Queen Elizabeth's Captain of the Guard. Even the Judges pitied him as they confirmed the sentence of death that had been so long suspended and now was to be executed. He had been, as the Chief Justice said, a dead man in the law for fifteen years 'and might at any minute have been cut off'. Yet a beheading seemed unnecessary. A natural end would take Raleigh's life soon enough without benefit of the axe and the block. 'He hath been as a star at which the world hath gazed,' the Attorney-General said – but stars must fall when they trouble the heavenly sphere.

King James signed the death warrant for an execution in the Old Palace Yard at Westminster the following day. The rush to kill him was a cautious policy, according to John Aubrey. It was contrived to

Old Palace Yard, Westminster. From an etching by Hollar, 1637.

take place on the Lord Mayor's Day so that 'pageants and fine shows might draw away the people from beholding the Tragedy of one of the most gallant worthies that ever England bred'. On his last evening on earth, Raleigh's wife Bess visited him and stayed until midnight. She sobbed and clung to him, but he said his farewell with his usual wit, telling her that she could now dispose of his body although she had not always been able to dispose of it when he was alive. After she was gone, he wrote a last business letter, a final defence of his actions for posterity, and a poem in the front of his Bible, his own epitaph.

> Even such is Time, which takes in trust
> Our Youth, our Joys, and all we have
> And pays us but with age and dust . . .

In the early hours of the morning, the Dean of Westminster came to give Raleigh spiritual advice and Holy Communion. Raleigh was calm, even cheerful. The Dean was surprised at his extraordinary boldness. Raleigh replied that he was innocent and so had no reason to behave as if he were guilty. The Dean reminded him that he had been condemned by the law, and that he had been an instrument in the death of Essex. Raleigh agreed that he had been sentenced under the law, but wrongly, and that Essex had been executed by a trick. He did not explain himself more. He ate a large breakfast and smoked a last pipe – to the Dean's dismay. He had been accused of smoking during Essex's execution, and now he was smoking just before his own. He had dressed shabbily for the past few months, but now he put on his best black clothes, satin and velvet and silk and taffeta breeches. He would be splendid at his final curtain.

He knew that what he did on this terminal stage would end the legend of his life. Given a cup of wine, he drank it, joking that it would taste good if he could delay to drink it. When an old bald man blessed him, Raleigh took off the lace cap under his hat and gave it away, saying that the bald man had 'more need of it now than I'. On the scaffold, he refused to warm himself by a fire and apologized to the crowd of watchers, saying that if he trembled, it would be from fever, not from fear. As his voice was no longer strong, the lords left their windows to come down to the scaffold and shake his hand and hear his final apology.

Raleigh denied all the charges against him, protested his loyalty to the King, and forgave all his enemies, even his cousin and betrayer Stukeley. Lord Arundel was asked if he had not heard Raleigh

A contemporary engraving of Sir Walter Raleigh on the scaffold with various lords.

promise to return to England whatever happened in Guiana. Arundel confirmed loudly that this was true. Then Raleigh brought up the subject of the execution of Essex. He denied that he had lit a pipe as Essex was beheaded and was sorrowful that he had not been on the scaffold to be reconciled with the condemned earl. He confessed that he had been Essex's enemy, but also that it was worse for him when Essex was gone. 'For those that set me up against him did afterwards set themselves against me, and were my greatest enemies.'

Raleigh now asked everyone to join him in a prayer, asking mercy for his sins. He had been too proud and vain. As a seafarer, a courtier and a soldier, he had been often tempted not to be a good man. He declared that he believed in the Church of England and hoped to be saved by the precious blood of our Saviour Jesus Christ. He now must say farewell, because he had to make a long journey.

The scaffold was cleared of Raleigh's friends and the lords. He gave away his fine outer clothes and asked to test the axe. He ran his thumb along its edge; his wit was as cutting as the blade. 'This is a sharp medicine,' he said, 'but it is a sure cure for all diseases.'

His courage and humour and self-possession moved all who saw him. His happiest hours, one observer wrote, were at his sentencing and his execution. He seemed more 'a spectator than a sufferer'. Even his enemies were forced to admire him. He pardoned the executioner, telling him to strike down when his victim stretched out his hands. He refused at first to kneel with his head facing east towards Jerusalem and salvation. 'So the heart be right,' he said, 'it is no matter which way the head lieth.' He also refused to be blindfolded. 'Think you I fear the shadow of the axe,' he declared, 'when I fear not the axe itself?'

After a final silent prayer, he put his head on the block and stretched out his hands. The executioner could not bring himself to strike. Raleigh put out his hands again. The executioner still could not move.

'What dost thou fear?' Raleigh said. 'Strike, man, strike.'

The executioner struck twice. He raised up Raleigh's severed head. The crowd shuddered as leaves in the wind. There was no cheering at the death of such a man.

XV

SEA-CHANGE

RALEIGH'S LIFE SAW A SEA-change. At his birth, the Mediterranean was still the focus of world trade and civilization. The Portuguese dominated the new trade routes to Africa and India and Asia, while the Spaniards had colonized Central and South America and also commanded the Atlantic and the Pacific Oceans. The encounter between Europe and the other continents of the world was through the people of the Iberian peninsula. Their Mediterranean culture was supreme, the only one known in the furthest ports of the globe. They were the ambassadors and the navigators, the traders and the bearers of Christian concepts to the outposts of the vast overseas empires granted to them by the Pope.

By the time of Raleigh's death, the Mediterranean was declining in influence, while the Iberian control of world trade was challenged by the English, the Dutch and the French, who were all beginning to found their own colonial empires. Their fleets rivalled the Iberian fleets and often overcame them. In his pride, Raleigh believed an English warship to be worth ten Spanish ones. He and his West Country relatives and friends were responsible for the beginnings of English overseas trade and colonization, particularly in North America and the Caribbean.

Before Raleigh took over Sir Humphrey Gilbert's royal letters patent, the thrust of English discovery was the search for a North-West Passage to China. Raleigh changed the direction, sending the first English colony to North Carolina, the forerunner of the successful colonies in Virginia and in Massachusetts, where the Pilgrims landed two years after his death. By his expeditions to Guiana, Raleigh also promoted the planting of colonies in the Caribbean: in his *Apology* for his last voyage, he listed all the benefits of living in the New World. 'Besides the excellent air, pleasantness, healthfullness, and riches, it hath plenty of corn, fruits, fishes, fowls, wild and tame, beeves, horse,

Observing the meridian altitude of the sun with an astrolabe, 1545.
From de Medina, Arte de Navegar.

sheep, hogs, deer, conies, hares, tortoises, armadilloes, bananas, oils, honey, wax, potatoes, sugarcanes, medicaments, balsam, gums, and what not.'

He pointed the way to the founding of the first British empire in North America and the Caribbean. He promoted it and finally paid with his life for it, at a time when the King wanted peace with Spain. Raleigh financed and organized many of the expeditions to the New

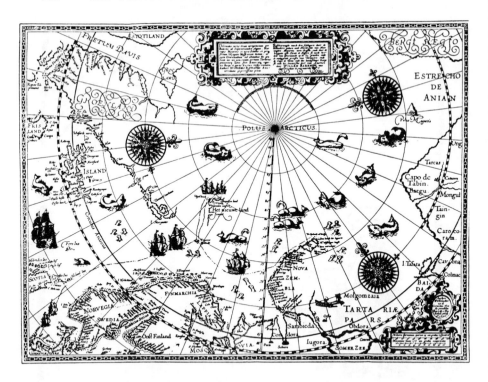

Barents's chart of the North, making the Davis Strait and the Strait of Anian the routes leading to China. From van Linschoten, Itinerario.

World, which led to the exchange of ideas and products between the original Americans and the forerunners of the English-speaking Americans. The naked natives first met by the Europeans grew in awareness and sophistication: the horse and the sheep, the gun and the axe transformed their lives as much as their gold and their potatoes and their tobacco changed the lives of European nations. If their technology was inferior to western technology, it was adapted to their forest lives. They built ingenious boats by hollowing and burning out tree-trunks – river craft superior to the coracles of the ancient Britons. And their techniques of fishing and hunting and farming provided food for the pioneer colonists, who had to learn from them how to live off the newly discovered land.

Brazilian Indians smoking tobacco and making fire before acquiring European matches and tinder boxes. From André Thevet, Les Singularités de la France Antarctique, autrement nommée Amérique, *1557.*

Raleigh preached the interdependence of peoples. In North Carolina, he perceived the mistakes made by the colonists in antagonizing the Indians. In Guiana, he advocated an alliance with the Indians, a cooperation for common benefit and resistance to tyrannous Spanish rule. He was astute enough to see that no colony would prosper without the support of the native inhabitants. Empire meant more than exploitation: it meant teaching and learning, the exchange of mutual aid – indeed, a commonwealth of nations.

Raleigh also contributed to the advancement of science and navigation, history and education. He was the patron and friend of experimental astronomers and chemists such as John Dee and Thomas Hariot. He encouraged the teaching of his sea captains in the skills of

American Indians burning out boats from hollowed logs. From Hariot,
A Brief and True Report . . ., *1589. By permission of the British Library.*

seamanship. He was himself a good chemist and doctor with a mind that enquired into everything under the sun and moon, taking nothing for granted. He would have examined the whole array of nature if he could, just as he explained the whole of human history as the workings of a divine providence that had led to his own remarkable life in such a momentous age.

Raleigh was a poet too. A dozen of his poems remain the ornaments of the English language. They have the brevity and the wit, the grace and the restless passion that distinguished the character of their author. Perhaps he described his own commitment to his quests and to the few people dear to him in the last verse of one of his best poems, 'As You Came From the Holy Land':

> But Love is a durable fire
> In the mind ever burning:
> Never sick, never old, never dead,
> From itself never turning.

Raleigh's example and legacy is his spirit of bold enquiry and dedicated endeavour. His considerable influence as a soldier and a sailor, a courtier and a royal adviser have made him known in history. But what shines out is the man himself in his richness and complexity.

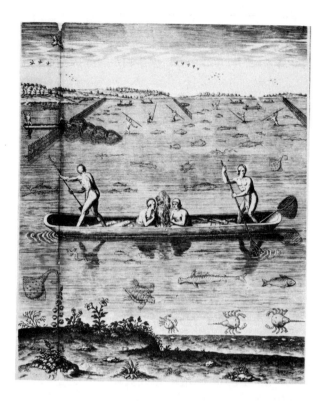

*John White's picture of American Indians fishing off Roanoke, North Carolina.
By permission of the British Library.*

To his enemies, he was a great Lucifer: to his friends, he seemed the silver knight of the Elizabethan age, daring and implacable in war, splendid and gracious at Court, persistent and searching in his mind, enduring and loving in his private life. His style was exceptional: he was at his best when his fortunes were at their worst. No other man would have the detached courage to be cheerful before his execution, so cheerful that a cousin reproached him for being 'too much upon the brave hand'.

Raleigh replied like the gallant he was. 'Give me leave to be merry for this is the last merriment that ever I shall have in this world. But when I come to the sad part, I will look on it like a man.'

An Elizabethan vessel.
From the frontispiece of William Bourne, A Regiment for the Sea, *1576.*

So he did, clear-sighted beneath the blade of the axe. His vision was the future, but his dreams were greater than his resources. He had a sense of theatre, in which he played the lead. He pursued his imagination to the limits of his powers and beyond. He knew that great things are only achieved by stretching mind and body to the furthest, even to the Valley of the Shadow of Death. There he rode, boldly rode, seeking for his El Dorado.

Without doubt, he was the guiding spirit behind the planting of the English-speaking peoples in North America and in the Caribbean during the Age of Discovery. He was the pioneer of that North Atlantic civilization that called the New World into existence to revive the hopes and energies of the Old. He was a patron of the inventive and enquiring minds that transformed English navigation and technology and chemistry in that other age of discovery of the nature of the planet and how to use it. His *History of the World* and the royal persecution of him made him into a hero and a martyr for those Members of Parliament who were to execute a King and make England, in the long term, a constitutional democracy that was to set the standard for the rest of mankind.

*A young Indian in Virginia, 1616. Already European sheep and goats
had been imported to change the livestock of North America. From an ink and wash
drawing by Brent de Bock. By permission of the Edinburgh University Library.*

Above all, the greatness of the man, the power of his foresight, the
bravery of his conduct, the quicksilver of his intellect, the grace of his
words, have made a legend of Sir Walter Raleigh. The romantic
Victorian painting by Sir John Millais of the young Raleigh listening
to the old salt telling of the new-found lands and the Edens beyond
the oceans captures something of the durable fire of that mind ever
burning to desire, to try, to fight, and never to give way – the
passionate pilgrim.

Operation Raleigh, 1984-1988

A GREAT EXPEDITION, OPERATION Raleigh, has been launched. It reaches as far as any of the expeditions of Sir Walter Raleigh. It will involve young people from around the world in scientific exploration and community service and will include over sixty separate expeditions; 4,000 Venturers from Britain, the U.S.A., and the rest of the world will take part. The first Venturers will set sail in November 1984 to Roanoke Island in North Carolina, where Raleigh sent the first English colony. This will coincide with celebrations to mark the 400th anniversary of the beginning of English-speaking America. From Roanoke the expedition will set out to circumnavigate the globe. It will visit thirty countries, where other Venturers will join the voyage of discovery. A scientific exploration vessel, the *Sir Walter Raleigh*, sponsored by the Hull City Council, will act as flagship, accompanied by other sailing ships, including square-riggers in the Caribbean and the Indian Ocean.

'The theme of Operation Raleigh,' its Patron, the Prince of Wales, says, 'is science and service.' It presents a unique opportunity and challenge to those Venturers who survive the rigorous selection procedure. It stands alone in the size and scope of its undertakings. Leading the expeditions will be some of the world's foremost scientists and explorers, such as Colonel John Blashford-Snell, Operations Director.

Any young person aged between sixteen and twenty-three may apply to be selected as a Venturer on Operation Raleigh. He or she must be able to speak English and to swim. Application forms are available from any branch of the Trustee Savings Bank, and from:

> The Selection Co-ordinator,
> Operation Raleigh,
> P.O. Box 370,
> Europe House,
> World Trade Centre,
> London E1 9AS

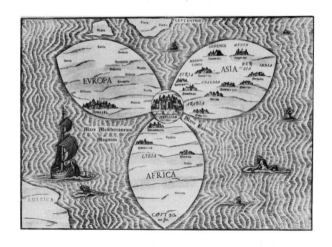

From the Renaissance Terrae Sanctae Tabula, *depicting Jerusalem as the centre of the continents of Europe, Africa and Asia. America is already known.*

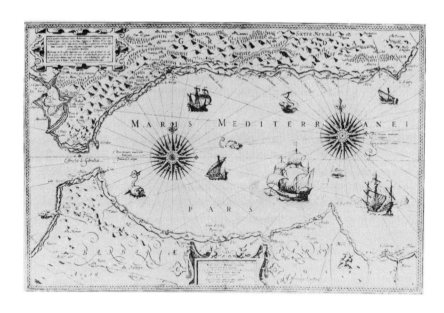

A printed chart of the Strait of Gibraltar, 1595,
showing full compass directions and coastal landmarks.
From William Barentzsoon's Description de la Mer Méditerranée.

CONTENTS

To Operation Raleigh and all who work for it

Penguin Books Ltd, Harmondsworth, Middlesex, England
Penguin Books, 40 West 23rd Street, New York, New York 10010, U.S.A.
Penguin Books Australia Ltd, Ringwood, Victoria, Australia
Penguin Books Canada Ltd, 2801 John Street, Markham, Ontario, Canada L3R 1B4
Penguin Books (N.Z.) Ltd, 182–190 Wairau Road, Auckland 10, New Zealand

First published 1984

Typeset, printed and bound in Great Britain by
Hazell Watson & Viney Limited,
Member of the BPCC Group,
Aylesbury, Bucks
Set in VIP Palatino

Andrew Sinclair

SIR WALTER RALEIGH

and the Age of Discovery

PENGUIN BOOKS

PENGUIN BOOKS

Sir Walter Raleigh and

Andrew Sinclair was born   I
Trinity College, Cambrid   er
The Breaking of Bumlo and *My Fri*
was in the United States as a Harkness Fellow of the
Commonwealth Fund. He studied American History at Harvard
and Columbia, and later took his Ph.D. at Cambridge in this
subject. He was director of Historical Studies at Churchill College,
Cambridge, from 1961 to 1963, and was a founding Fellow of the
College. In the following year he was made a Fellow of the
American Council of Learned Societies. He returned to England
to teach at University College, London.

His other novels include *Gog* (1968) and its sequel *Magog*
(1972); he is currently working on the third volume of the trilogy,
King Ludd. He has also written *Prohibition: the Era of Excess* and
The Better Half: the Emancipation of the American Woman, which won
a Somerset Maugham Award, as well as several biographies,
including ones on Jack London, John Ford, and *The Other Victoria*,
Empress of Germany. He frequently appears on television and
radio as a critic and is a Fellow of the Royal Literary Society and
of the Society of American Historians.